ACTS 13-20
GROWTH
OF THE BODY

RAY STEDMAN

**VISION HOUSE
PUBLISHERS**
Santa Ana, California 92705

Copyright ©1976 by Vision House Publishers
Santa Ana, California 92705

Library of Congress Catalog Number 76-47845
ISBN 0-88449-059-9

The Scripture quotations in this publication are from the
Revised Standard Version Bible, copyright 1946, 1952, © and
1971 and 1973 by the Division of Christian Education,
National Council of the Churches of Christ in the U.S.A., and
used by permission.

Printed in the United States of America.

CONTENTS

INTRODUCTION

God has always made the Middle East the focal point of history and of current events. With the intensification of developments there since the Jews returned to Israel, events have now come full circle. This is where Christianity began, where the explosion of the gospel first occurred. In the Book of Acts we have the joyful account of how this radical gospel broke out on a decadent, pagan society, capturing the interest and the hearts of men, awakening hope in a hopeless world, and changing lives by a fundamental transformation of behavior and outlook.

In its original form as a series of messages, this section of Acts was titled "The Pattern Setters," because this is the account of the missionary journeys of the Apostle Paul, during which a pattern was laid down for Christian witness in any age. Through Luke's eyes we can trace the establishment of the church in many places, but, equally important, we can see how the early Christians grew in numbers and spread their influence throughout the world around them.

Various elements of truth appear again and again on these pages, and this repetition shows the importance of these truths to the church today. The church is intended to live in the atmosphere of the Book of Acts and to manifest its accomplishments throughout its whole history. Whenever the church has not done so, it has been because this pattern was neglected. Surely nothing could be more important today than for the church to return to the blueprint of power which the Book of Acts presents.

CHAPTER ONE

THE STRATEGY OF
THE SPIRIT

Acts 13:1-13

The thirteenth chapter of the Book of Acts is what Winston Churchill would have called a "hinge of history." It marks the beginning of the third phase of our Lord's Great Commission. In the opening chapter of this book, before he ascended into the heavens, Jesus had said to his disciples, "You shall receive power when the Holy Spirit has come upon you; and you shall be my witnesses . . ." (Acts 1:8). Then he outlined geographically how that witness should proceed—beginning in Jerusalem, then in Judea and Samaria, and finally unto the uttermost parts of the earth. In Acts 13 we have the beginning of the last phase, the going unto the uttermost parts of the earth.

This chapter also records the beginning of the apostleship of Paul. Although he was called to be an apostle when he was first converted on the Damascus road, he had so far never acted as an apostle. Now, some eleven or twelve years after his conversion, he begins to fulfill the ministry to which he was called as an apostle of Jesus Christ.

But perhaps the most important thing contained in this section is the revelation of the ways in which the

Spirit of God guides his people. The first three verses relate the call of the Holy Spirit:

> **Now in the church at Antioch there were prophets and teachers, Barnabas, Symeon who was called Niger, Lucius of Cyrene, Manaen a member of the court of Herod the tetrarch, and Saul. While they were worshipping the Lord and fasting, the Holy Spirit said, "Set apart for me Barnabas and Saul for the work to which I have called them." Then after fasting and praying they laid their hands on them and sent them off" (Acts 13:1-3).**

Notice that the whole event begins with a group of Christians in the church at Antioch who are exercising the spiritual gifts that were given to them. Certain prophets and teachers are mentioned—men who had the gift of prophecy, and others who had the gift of teaching. In the Greek text it is clear that three of the men were prophets and two were teachers.

The first three were prophets. Barnabas we know as the person who vouched for the newly converted Saul before the skeptical and fearful disciples. Symeon (who was called Niger, a reference to the area of Africa now known as Nigeria, indicating that perhaps this man was a black) was very likely the same Symeon (Simon) who was forced by the Romans to bear the cross of Jesus when he fell under its weight on his way to the crucifixion. Lucius, from Cyrene (located in Africa along the Mediterranean coast), was perhaps also black and was the third prophet.

Then there were two teachers, Manaen and Saul. Manaen was a member of the court of Herod the tetrarch. This is not the Herod whose death is recorded in Chapter 12; this is the Herod before whom our Lord appeared, and at whose hands he suffered. Manaen was related to Herod as a foster brother and was thus very close to the king. These men are a collection, then, of people from all walks of life: Symeon, a black man; Lucius, perhaps also black; Barnabas, a man from the island of Cyprus; and Manaen, a nobleman from the aristocratic class of society.

With them was Saul of Tarsus. The amazing thing here is that he is listed only as a teacher. He is not called an apostle, nor even a prophet; he is a teacher in the church at Antioch. At this point in his career the only gift that was visible in his life was his wonderful ability to teach the Word of God.

Using Their Gifts

While these men were using their gifts, busy doing what God had equipped them to do in the church, the Spirit of God spoke to them. I think this is very significant, because many people today are confused and uncertain about the circumstances under which God will lead them. They think they must hole up in a cave or isolate themselves with nature in order to hear God speak. Once they get away on a mountain somewhere they expect him to speak in some dramatic fashion and send them back with a great sense of personal calling. But God does not often call people in this way. Usually his call comes when we are busy exercising our gift where we are, just as these men were. It was in the midst of their activity that the call of the Spirit came.

We don't know exactly how the Spirit spoke to these men. It may have been in a prophetic utterance through one of the prophets. Or it may well have been that he spoke as he speaks to many people today in what has been termed "insistent unanimity," a deep conviction shared by everyone in the group that the Spirit of God desires a certain thing. This is often the way God works. At any rate, he spoke to men who were already at work doing what they knew—that is the point! You can steer a ship or a car if it is moving, but it is very difficult to steer when it is sitting still.

Notice also two elements of the Spirit's sovereign choice. He chose the *men*, and he chose the *work*. He said, "Separate unto me Barnabas and Saul for the work to which I have called them." He didn't tell the church what that work was (although he had told Barnabas and Saul), and we don't find out what it was until we read on and see what they did. But the Spirit had spoken to these men and had laid on them a deep concern to reach out to the world around; then he said to the church, "Now set them aside for this purpose." That is the way the call of God came in this initial thrusting out toward the uttermost parts of the earth.

I want to comment on one other thing here, and that is that the believers were all fasting. This was not because they were overweight; it was because they were concerned. In the Bible, fasting is always the mark of deep spiritual concern. It means that a person is willing to set aside his normal demands of life in order to concentrate for a time on finding what God wants, and to pray that what he wants will be accomplished. It is too bad that fasting has largely disappeared from the Christian church, because it is a very helpful and very needed expression of spiritual awareness. As these men were concerned about what God wanted to do, they met together, foregoing food for a time and exercising their gifts. When the Spirit of God spoke to them, the whole church recognized it and identified themselves with these two men as they went out.

Then after fasting and praying they laid their hands on them and sent them off.

This means that the whole church was involved as one body, acting together to indicate to these men that they would support them in prayer and provide whatever financial support they needed to fulfill their ministry. As they went out, they had this expression of the unity and harmony of the whole church behind them. That is the body at work, and what a beautiful picture it is.

Sovereignty and Responsibility

But we also see a wonderful blending of the sovereignty of the Spirit and the responsibility of men. Look at this next section:

So, being sent out by the Holy Spirit, they went down to Seleucia; and from there they sailed to Cyprus. When they arrived at Salamis, they proclaimed the word of God in the synagogues of the Jews. And they had John to assist them (Acts 13:4, 5).

God's sovereign, authoritative choice is expressed in the sending out of these men by the Holy Spirit. It was the Spirit who laid this on their hearts and created in them an intense desire to move out. But then the next phrase reads, "They went down to Seleucia; and from there they sailed to Cyprus." The Spirit did not tell them to go to Cyprus; that was the choice of Saul and Barnabas. The Spirit told them to move out, but the men decided where to go.

This is perfectly proper. Paul and Barnabas were acting in confidence that the Spirit was not only thrusting them out, but was also working in them to decide where to go. As Paul wrote later to the Philippians, "Work out your own salvation [solutions] with fear and trembling; for God is at work in you, both to will and to work for his good pleasure" (Phil. 2:12, 13). When they thought over the situation they decided that Cyprus would be the logical place to start. They didn't wait for the Spirit to point it out on the map; they decided on the basis of the natural contacts they had. Barnabas was from Cyprus, and so were the men who started the church at Antioch. They undoubtedly had many contacts there, so that is where they started. But they went with the confidence that God was in their choice.

This is the way to be led of the Spirit. The Spirit may lay on your heart some need, some ministry, some opportunity that is before you, so that you feel impressed to do it, and perhaps others will join you in it. But if you don't know quite how to get started, begin with what looks like the most natural thing, being confident that God is in you to govern and lead you in your choice, and to bring out of it what he wants.

Note also that when Paul and Barnabas arrived at Salamis, they began in the synagogues. Why did they start there? Was it because they were Jews and they knew that other Jews who had the Scriptures would listen to them? Was it simply the most natural place to start? Yes, that is true, but I don't think this is the whole reason. We are not told as much in this text, but in the Epistle to the Romans we learn that it was revealed to Paul that the gospel was first to go to the Jews and then to the Gentiles. Everywhere he went, Paul began with the Jews. Again we see the combination of natural reasons *and* the specific and precise command of the Holy Spirit. Paul always followed this pattern: he went to the Jews first, and when they rejected the message he went to the Gentiles.

On this journey Paul and Barnabas took an intern with them, a young man whose name was John Mark. Mark was not commanded of the Lord to go with them, but Saul and Barnabas chose him, and in their choice we see the human element once more.. Mark had a rich mother who could aid in their financial expense, and he was also Barnabas' cousin. So they simply followed natural lines of choice in their decision to take young John Mark, the one who later wrote the Gospel according to Mark.

Expecting the Unexpected

As the men preached on Cyprus they obviously expected God to be with them and to open doors everywhere they went. This is the way the Holy Spirit commonly operates; we are not to wait for orders concerning everything we do. Young Christians often get the idea that they are to be like robots, automatons, ruled by computer-impulses which come from the Spirit, and that they must sit and wait until such an impulse comes. While I was a student at Dallas Seminary I remember a young man who thought this was the way the Spirit worked. He would stop at the foot of a staircase and ask God to show him whether he should go up the right side or the left. He would pray about whether to put his hat on in the morning, or not.

If God ran our lives like that we would be nothing more than mechanical beings. Animals are controlled in that way, by their instincts, but not men. God wants us to understand that he lives within us. He *will* direct us precisely at times, and when he does we must not ignore his direction. But when he doesn't we are to move out where we are with the confident expectation that God is with us and will open the doors to make a way for us. When we follow that pattern, life becomes exciting. God is infinitely creative, always doing something surprising, unexpected.

You cannot improve upon the strategy of the Holy Spirit. No one could anticipate the right way to approach these Cyprian cities. One of the problems with the church in the twentieth century is that we are forever calling conventions, councils, retreats, and conferences to try to decide where we ought to go next. We devise programs, structuring and organizing God's work along carefully planned lines, as though the whole thing depended on us. This is one reason the church is faltering in so many places, and why it has lost its note of excitement. The strategy belongs to the Holy Spirit. He is the only one who knows how to reach a city or a county or a nation. As Paul and Barnabas discovered, he already had men planted here and there, ready to respond whenever his people go out to proclaim the truth.

I heard a wonderful example recently of how the Holy Spirit works along this line. A friend told me that the Christian World Liberation Front was trying to do something about the topless and bottomless bars in San Francisco. They organized a protest and started walking up and down in front of some of these lewd, lurid places, carrying signs—rather ironic signs—such as, THURSDAY NIGHT IS FAMILY NIGHT . . . BRING THE

CHILDREN TO EL CONDOR. Customers became so embarrassed by these signs that they stopped entering the bars.

Finally the management, angered by the marked decrease in attendance, sent out a bouncer to order the Christians off the sidewalk. But these Christians, knowing they had a right to orderly protest, refused to leave. One night the bouncer got very angry and hit one of the leaders right in the mouth. But the Christians were back again the next night, not knowing how to proceed, but counting on the Lord.

This time the bouncer came out and ordered them to go, but they said they wouldn't leave unless they could go in and pray for the people first. Surprisingly, the management agreed and invited them in. The place was absolutely dead silent as these Christians stood up on the stage, surrounded by naked girls, and led the whole place in prayer. One fellow said he peeked while the rest were praying and saw the bouncer going around quietly closing all the doors so they wouldn't be disturbed by any noise from the street. They had a tremendous opportunity to speak the truth to these people, who became utterly different in their demeanor when they were confronted with this kind of a contrast between the right and the wrong.

We find this kind of radicalism of the Holy Spirit all through the Book of Acts. We are colaborers with God, and when we work together with him in this way he produces exciting situations and climactic circumstances which almost always open the door for a fruitful ministry.

Luke doesn't tell us everything Paul and Barnabas did as they went through the Island of Cyprus in this way. They must have had a very effective ministry, however, because Christian churches were established in

Cyprus right from the beginning. The one incident in Cyprus that is recorded for us is given for a special reason. Luke tells us that Paul and Barnabas worked their way across the island from east to west, probably visiting all the cities along the way. After perhaps two or three months they finally arrived at Paphos, the capital of the island on the western shore, where an unusual event took place:

> When they had gone through the whole island as far as Paphos, they came upon a certain magician, a Jewish false prophet, named Bar-jesus. He was with the proconsul, Sergius Paulus, a man of intelligence, who summoned Barnabas and Saul and sought to hear the word of God. But Elymas the magician (for that is the meaning of his name) withstood them, seeking to turn away the proconsul from the faith (Acts 13:6-8).

Here is a remarkable example of how the Holy Spirit works. Paul and Barnabas had no idea that they would be able to speak to the governor of the island, the proconsul. This man had been placed there by the Roman senate and was responsible for the control and governance of the whole island. But this proconsul, prompted by the Holy Spirit even though he was a pagan Roman, sent for Paul and Barnabas and asked them to speak to him the words of truth. So Paul and Barnabas came and began to preach to the governor.

It is interesting that archeology has confirmed Luke's report. Inscriptions bearing the name of this very governor, Sergius Paulus, have been found in Cyprus. Furthermore, Sir William Ramsey had uncovered evidence that he was a Christian and that his whole family became

Christians and were very prominent in Christian circles after this event.

Crooked Paths

When Paul and Barnabas began to teach Sergius Paulus, they were opposed by a Jewish magician whose professional name was Elymas, which means "magician." His name in Hebrew was Bar-Jesus, and from this we get a hint of what this man was doing. Bar-Jesus means "the son of Jesus." In the Hebrew culture, to call yourself a son of someone was to designate yourself his follower. When this man called himself Bar-Jesus, therefore, he was claiming to be a follower of Jesus, but what he taught was absolutely contrary to the teachings of Jesus. He was, in other words, the first in a long line of Christian cultists who seize upon the name of Jesus and the name of Christianity as a guise for utterly unchristian teaching. Many have followed him, so that today we have Mormonism, Jehovah's Witnesses, and many new sects which claim the name of Christianity but teach the most unchristian doctrines.

Because this man was such a fraud, he very greatly provoked the spirit of Paul:

> But Saul, who is also called Paul, filled with the Holy Spirit, looked intently at him and said, "You son of the devil, you enemy of all righteousness, full of all deceit and villainy, will you not stop making crooked the straight paths of the Lord?" (Acts 13:9, 10).

Do you see what was happening? Paul was declaring the straight paths of Jesus, but this man was teaching deviations, thus misleading this proconsul. So Paul said, in these rather blunt and direct words, "You son of the devil, you enemy of all righteousness, full of all deceit and villainy, you had better stop what you're doing, perverting the straight paths of the Lord."

First Sign of Apostleship

Then he did a very significant thing:

"And now, behold, the hand of the Lord is upon you, and you shall be blind and unable to see the sun for a time." Immediately mist and darkness fell upon him and he went about seeking people to lead him by the hand. Then the proconsul believed, when he saw what had occurred, for he was astonished at the teaching of the Lord (Acts 13:11, 12).

Why was this event selected out of the ministry at Cyprus and recorded for us as the one significant occurrence of that ministry? It is because it was here that Paul began to act as an apostle: "filled with the Holy Spirit," he began for the first time to fulfil his apostolic calling. This is the first of those "signs of an apostle" which Paul fulfilled in order to indicate that he was selected by the Lord Jesus to be a founder of the church, empowered to lay the foundation of faith and become a writer of Scriptures. Note that Paul speaks to Elymas with the same authority that Peter manifested when Ananias and Sapphira attempted to pose as pious frauds, as recorded in the fifth chapter of Acts. In both cases there was an immediate judgment. Only the apostles had the power to bring about such immediate judgments; this is not something which just any Christian can do.

Paul has now become an apostle, and the leadership shifts immediately from Barnabas to Paul. From here on it is no longer *Barnabas and Saul* but *Paul and Barnabas,* as verse 13 confirms:

Now *Paul and his company* set sail from Paphos, and came to Perga in Pamphylia.

This event, then, is the beginning of the great ministry of the Apostle Paul, and the primary characteristic of that ministry was his power in teaching. What impressed this proconsul was not the miracle, for this simply confirmed what he had heard. What impressed him and made him believe was the teaching of the Lord, the remarkable, radical doctrine of Christianity: Jesus Christ the Son of God has become man and is prepared to live his life again in every human being who will receive him.

Dear Father, make us obedient followers of the strategy of the Spirit and careful teachers of this most revolutionary truth. Our age needs this as desperately as did the first century. Make us faithful imitators of Paul as he was of Christ. In Christ's name, Amen.

CHAPTER TWO

THE RADICAL WORD

Acts 13:13-52

The Apostle Paul has changed the course of world history by the power of his ministry in the Spirit of Christ. He did so by the preaching of the Word of truth, and in the latter part of Acts 13 we have a good example of how he did it. Paul had preached many times before, but this powerful and shattering message is the first of which we have a record. It was given in a synagogue on a sabbath morning and it shook a whole city—so much so that in verse 44 of this account we read, "The next sabbath almost the whole city gathered together to hear the word of God."

We need to examine Paul's message in some detail to see why it made such an impact then, and what elements make it radical and revolutionary even today. This message is not preached as widely as it needs to be today, perhaps because people do not often want to hear the gospel presented as it is given in the Scriptures.

John Mark Turns Back

We left Paul, Barnabas, and young John Mark on the island of Cyprus at Paphos, the capital city. They were about to sail across the arm of the Mediterranean to Asia Minor, and Luke now resumes the account for us at verse 13:

> **Now Paul and his company set sail from Paphos, and came to Perga in Pamphylia. And John left them and returned to Jerusalem; but they passed on from Perga and came to Antioch of Pisidia. And on the sabbath day they went into the synagogue and sat down. After the reading of the law and the prophets, the rulers of the synagogue sent to them, saying, "Brethren, if you have any word of exhortation for the people, say it" (Acts 13:13-15).**

As we have already pointed out, the subtle shift from "Barnabas and Saul" to "Paul and his company" marks the beginning of the apostleship of Paul, and of his leadership of this missionary journey. It may also suggest at least one reason why, as Luke records in the next sentence, young John Mark left them and went back to Jerusalem. As the cousin of Barnabas, Mark may well have resented this change in leadership. There is some indication in the Scriptures that he and Paul did not get along too well, at least at first. Later on Paul will write from prison in Rome and ask that Mark be sent to him, as he is of great profit to him by then.

But now there seems to be a great deal of friction. John Mark was the son of a wealthy widow, raised in luxury. There is some evidence that he was the rich young ruler who refused to follow Jesus because he had many possessions. If that is so, he has by this time returned and become a follower of Jesus. But some scholars feel that he was afraid of the hardships that were developing on this journey. The three men were coming into the rugged mainland where paganism was rampant, where robbers and other dangers were on every hand, and where they faced increasing opposition from religious leaders. Mark may well have weakened at this point and, resenting the leadership of Paul, returned to Jerusalem.

So Paul and Barnabas went on to Antioch. This is not the Antioch in Syria, which they left to go to Cyprus, but another Antioch in the region of Pisidia, which was part of the ancient Roman province of Galatia. When you read Paul's Letter to the Galatians, you are reading a letter written to the Christians in the cities which were reached on this first missionary journey: Antioch, Iconium, Lystra, and Derbe.

They came into the synagogue, according to the pattern which Paul always followed. It was the custom in the synagogue for strangers to be invited to speak, and what these Jews heard from Paul was of very great importance. This speech falls into three simple divisions which we will look at very carefully so as to understand the power of this mighty word.

> So Paul stood up, and motioning with his hand said: "Men of Israel, and you that fear God, listen. The God of this people Israel chose our fathers and made the people great during their stay in the land of Egypt, and with uplifted arm he led them out of it. And for about forty years he bore with them in the wilderness. And when he had destroyed seven nations in the land of Canaan, he gave them their land as an inheritance, for about four hundred and fifty years. And after that he gave them judges until Samuel the prophet. Then they asked for a king; and God gave them Saul the son of Kish, a man of the tribe of Benjamin, for forty years. And when he had removed him, he raised up David to be their king; of

whom he testified and said, 'I have found in David the son of Jesse a man after my heart, who will do all my will.' Of this man's posterity God has brought to Israel a Savior, Jesus, as he promised. Before his coming John had preached a baptism of repentance to all the people of Israel. And as John was finishing his course, he said, 'What do you suppose that I am? I am not he. No, but after me one is coming, the sandals of whose feet I am not worthy to untie' " (Acts 13:16-25).

Perhaps you have noticed that the introduction is in the same style as Stephen's great message recorded in the seventh chapter of Acts. Stephen had stood before the Sanhedrin, of which Saul of Tarsus was a member, and had recounted the history of Israel in order to try to awaken these stubborn Jews to an understanding of God's love and concern, and of his sovereign direction of their nation. Paul never forgot the power of that message. It had reached to his own heart, had cut through all the bigotry and egotism, and had planted a seed of faith in his heart which was ultimately to result in his conversion. So here he is following the same tactics as Stephen.

True History

But notice that though this introduction is history, it is not history as we usually read it. Most of the history books I have read center upon certain men—men who have done various deeds, either great or foul. Men like Adolf Hitler, or George Washington, or Winston Churchill—outstanding personalities—men with what the world calls "charisma," who leave their mark upon an age. But you will notice that this history centers on *God*; it is God who is working. This is history as it ought to be written, because it is history as it really was. The apostle points out eleven different instances of God's work in history: God chose the fathers, made the people great, led them out of Egypt, bore with them in the wilderness, destroyed seven nations in the land of Canaan, gave them their land, gave them judges, gave them Saul for a king, removed Saul, raised up David, and finally, "God has brought to Israel a Savior, Jesus, as he promised." It all culminates in the coming of the Lord Jesus himself.

Then Paul cites John's testimony to the greatness of Jesus. This was a telling blow because out in the provinces, away from Jerusalem, John the Baptist was regarded as a great prophet. So here Paul quotes his testimony to the fact that the person who was coming after him was so great that John himself said he was not worthy to untie his shoe. That is the introduction.

In the second division of Paul's message we have the timeless facts of the gospel: the ministry, the crucifixion, and the resurrection of Jesus:

> **Brethren, sons of the family of Abraham, and those among you that fear God, to us has been sent the message of this salvation. For those who live in Jerusalem and their rulers, because they did not recognize him nor understand the utterances of the prophets which are read every sabbath, fulfilled these by condemning him. Though they could charge him with nothing deserving death, yet they asked Pilate to have him killed. And when they had fulfilled all that was written of him, they took him down from the tree, and laid him in a tomb. But God**

raised him from the dead; and for many days he appeared to those who came up with him from Galilee to Jerusalem, who are now his witnesses to the people (Acts 13:26-31).

I recently read an article by a very prominent liberal theologian of our day, in which he said it was almost impossible to define the gospel clearly. But Paul did not have any such trouble; to him the gospel was very clear. It consisted of the great acts of God in history, the coming of the Lord Jesus, his ministry among men, his crucifixion because of the sins of men, and his resurrection as the Scriptures had promised. In First Corinthians he puts it this way:

Now I would remind you, brethren, in what terms I preached to you the gospel. . . . For I delivered to you as of first importance what I also received, that Christ died for our sins in accordance with the scriptures, that he was buried, that he was raised on the third day in accordance with the scriptures (1 Cor. 15:1, 3, 4).

This is the Good News, the basis for everything God does, and here Paul makes that very, very clear indeed.

If Jesus Was Messiah . . .

Here also, Paul gives us the answer to a question that many people are still asking today: how is it, if Jesus was the Messiah predicted by the Old Testament Scriptures, and if he fulfilled these when he came, that the Jews did not recognize him? Paul says there were two reasons. First, they did not really see Jesus. They were misled by superficialities about him. They looked at his trade and his background and saw that he was only a carpenter's son. They saw that he had no money or influence or standing in society. They saw that he had no prestige—he had never been to school, had never been taught at a great scholar's feet—so they wrote him off and paid no attention to him. They didn't hear his words, and they didn't see his miracles—or if they did, they immediately forgot them. Jesus lived the most magnificent life that had ever been lived before men, but his contemporaries never saw it; "they did not recognize him."

A lot of people are blind in this way today, like the Jews, because of the second reason: they did not understand the Scriptures. Here were people who had heard the utterances of the Prophets read to them every Saturday in the synagogue. They knew many of them by heart, but they didn't understand them. The reason they didn't understand is that they never asked any questions. They didn't take the Scriptures seriously. The reading of the Scriptures had become just a religious rite, a perfunctory performance. People went and did their thing in synagogue, and then went home again. Because of this they missed the coming of the Son of God and failed to recognize him as the Messiah. And so, as Paul says, they fulfilled the prophecies by condemning Jesus and turning him over to Pilate.

The Promises Fulfilled

In the third division of his message, Paul takes the two great truths of the ministry of Jesus and his resurrection and nails them down for these Jews by quoting the Scriptures to them:

And we bring you the good news that what God promised to the fathers, this he has fulfilled to us their children by raising Jesus. . . . (Acts 13:32, 33a).

(This does not mean raising him from the dead. It is an expression very much like the one in verse 22, "he raised up David," which does not mean that David was resurrected but that he was brought into office. God also raised up Jesus, that is, brought him into humanity.)

. . . as also it is written in the second psalm,
"Thou art my Son,
today I have begotten thee" (Acts 13:33b).

The promise in Psalm 2 was that the Son of God would be begotten as a man and would come into humanity. Then the second fact:

And as for the fact that he raised him from the dead, no more to return to corruption, he spoke in this way,
"I will give you the holy and sure blessings of David."
Therefore he says also in another psalm,
"Thou wilt not let thy Holy One see corruption (Acts 13:34, 35).

Psalm 16 clearly predicted the coming of a man who would never see corruption, whose body would not decay, would not disintegrate in the grave. Regarding psalms of this type, certain skeptics say, "These psalms don't refer to Jesus; they are just referring to experiences in David's life. David wrote this psalm; therefore it pertains to him. We just don't have the record of it, but he is talking about some unknown experience of his own." Many of the prophetic psalms are discounted on that basis. Psalm 22, which so beautifully describes the crucifixion, and which even opens with the words of Jesus on the cross, "My God, my God, why hast thou forsaken me?" is often minimized as being but an experience of David. But here Paul answers that type of argument before it can even be raised. He says,

For David, after he had served the counsel of God in his own generation, fell asleep, and was laid with his fathers, and saw corruption; but he whom God raised up saw no corruption (Acts 13:36, 37).

In other words, you cannot apply Psalm 16 to David, for it points to someone who would come later, of the lineage of David, who would never see corruption when he died. Witnesses saw Jesus alive after he died; he saw no corruption. Thus Paul confirms the fact of Christ's resurrection.

Now we come to the heart of the message; here is the hammer blow of this word:

Let it be known to you therefore, brethren, that through this man forgiveness of sins is proclaimed to you, and by him every one that believes is freed from everything from which you could not be freed by the law of Moses (Acts 13:38, 39).

This was a shattering statement. Here were men who honored the law of Moses, who thought the Ten Commandments were the greatest word that God had ever given to men. They were trying their best to live up to them in one way or another, and many of them realized they were failing. But they still thought the way to God was to obey the Ten Commandments, to try their best to be good. But now Paul comes to declare to them that they will never find acceptance with God in that way. You cannot be accepted by God on the basis of trying to be good. The Ten Commandments will not help you a bit; they will condemn you, because you will not fulfill them, no matter how hard you try!

What the Law Could Not Do

Rather, Paul tells the people, God has found a way to accept mankind even though man cannot be good enough in himself, and that way is through this man, Jesus Christ. Today we are accustomed to hearing this; it doesn't shake us. But perhaps you can imagine how it shook these people. They had never heard anything like this before, this amazing news that God would accept them. Unfortunately, our version somewhat diminishes its impact because it uses the term "freed." Paul really says, "Every one that believes is *justified* from everything from which you could not be justified by the law of Moses." This is the first recorded occasion of Paul's use of that great word which is so frequent in the Book of Romans, "justification by faith."

What does it mean to be justified? Most people think it means to have your sins forgiven, which is true, but it means a great deal more than this. Justification means to have your sins forgiven *in such a way that God's honor and integrity are preserved.* Let me use a term which explains this very well, although it is not theological. After serving in the Navy for two years, I was honorably discharged. My being discharged meant that I was through. The Navy had no further claim on me, nor I any relationship to them. But what I liked about this event was the word "honorable." It was an *honorable* discharge. I could freely show my discharge papers to anyone. There was no blot or stain on my discharge. As far as the Navy was concerned I had behaved well (there were some things they didn't know) and thus I was honorably discharged. But I knew certain men in the Navy, because I worked in the legal office, who were dishonorably discharged. They were just as separate from the Navy as I. The Navy was just as through with them as it was with me. But there was a blot on their discharge; they did not like to show their discharge papers to anyone. In fact, their dishonorable discharge could even affect their employment.

So what Paul is really saying here is this: If God forgave in the way most people think he does, if he were to say concerning our sin, "Oh, forget about it, that's all right, don't worry about it; you're such a great fellow and I love you so much that I'm just going to ignore it," then God's honor would be impugned. His character would be defiled by that kind of forgiveness. He could no longer be regarded as the God of justice and truth; he would be a partaker in my sins and yours.

But God has found a way, through Jesus, to lay the guilt of our life and heart upon his own Son. Thus he has preserved his honor and character and integrity, and at the same time he has been free to show his whole love to us. That is justification. Because of the cross nobody will ever be able to point to God and say, "Aha! You let people off who are guilty!" In the cross of Jesus God poured out all his judgment upon his Son. And in that cross, in the agony and the anguish of it, the world can see a picture of how faithfully God obeys his own laws and carries out justice to the nth degree. And yet, the wonder of it all is that God's love is therefore freed to be poured out to *us*, so that the result of justification is *full acceptance*. If you accept the death of the Lord Jesus on your behalf, and his life is given to you, you are justified from all things. Isn't this a great word? It means that God's unqualified love is poured out toward you. There is no rejection whatsoever, for any cause. God's love begins to heal all your scars and hurt and anguish, and you start becoming a whole person—all on the basis of being justified by faith.

This kind of love is incredible! Again and again I run across people who shake their heads and say, "That can't be; I've got to do *something*. The only way God can find me acceptable is for me to make myself acceptable." But no one can ever make himself acceptable to God by trying to live a good life. Many people find this truth difficult to accept, but that is the radical character of this great concept!

A Moment of Crisis

Paul evidently saw some frowns as he spoke, because he immediately adds these words:

> **Beware, therefore, lest there come upon you what is said in the prophets:**
> "**Behold, you scoffers, and wonder, and perish;**
> **for I do a deed in your days, a deed you will**
> **never believe, if one declares it to you**"
> (**Acts 13:40, 41**).

I don't think these words were spoken in sharpness, but in sadness. The apostle is saying here that when you hear this incredible word of grace—that God has found a way to love you without qualification—this is a moment of crisis in your life. You can either accept it and live in the glory of that love, or you can reject it and turn away. But if you reject it, you will find yourself in tremendous danger: you are in danger both of destroying yourself and of being destroyed, because only God's love can rescue man!

This was sharply underlined for me a few years ago. Sitting in my church study one weekday morning I suddenly heard a woman's voice shouting and crying out. I came out to see what was wrong, and I found a young married woman whom I had talked with the week before, walking up and down in front of the cross above the platform. She was looking up at the cross and crying, "Yes, there *is* a God; *yes*, there is a God and he *will* forgive me—I know he will! I know he will!" She was in torment of spirit.

I didn't know what to make of it for a moment. I listened to her, and then I moved to speak to her. When she saw me she just crumpled and fell on her face to the floor. I picked her up and helped her to a pew, and we talked together. The previous week she told me that although she was married and although she professed to be a Christian, she was having an affair with an older man. She had justified it, thinking it was something that would contribute to her happiness. I had tried to help her gently and patiently and lovingly. I didn't condemn her, but sought to help her see what she was doing to herself.

Then, this day, the man had called her and told her he was through. It shattered her, and, crushed with guilt, she came trying to find release. Suddenly it had dawned on her what she had done to her family, what she had done to her husband, what she had done to herself, how she had hurt everyone. She came trying to find forgiveness, crying out to God. But I could see as I talked with her that she didn't really believe the forgiveness that was offered. I went through the Scriptures with her, but she refused to accept God's forgiveness. She felt that somehow she must do something, she must atone. She would not believe what God had said: that there is no condemnation to those who are in Christ Jesus, that he would freely forgive and wash it all away, and that then, in the strength of his healing, wholeness would follow.

Finally she calmed down a bit. She called her husband and he came over. I talked with them, and then he took her home. But she was still distressed, so her husband took her to the hospital. Two days later I received word that in her anguish of mind she had thrown herself from the tenth floor of the hospital and her body was crushed on the pavement below.

That is the awful pressure of guilt. If you do not find a way to relieve it, it will destroy you! And that is why this message hit with such power in this city. Paul laid out before them the fact that the only way, the *only* way, to be freed from guilt is to accept the work of Another on your behalf. God's love is unqualifiedly poured out on that basis, and that alone.

Either Faith or Jealousy

Now look at the results of this message:

As they went out, the people begged that these things might be told them the next sabbath. And when the meeting of the synagogue broke up, many Jews and devout converts to Judaism followed Paul and Barnabas, who spoke to them and urged them to continue in the grace of God.

The next sabbath almost the whole city gathered
together to hear the word of God. But when the Jews
saw the multitudes, they were filled with jealousy,
and contradicted what was spoken by Paul, and
reviled him. And Paul and Barnabas spoke out boldly, saying, "It was necessary that the word of God
should be spoken first to you. Since you thrust it
from you, and judge yourselves unworthy of eternal
life, behold, we turn to the Gentiles. For so the Lord
has commanded us, saying,
　　'I have set you to be a light for the Gentiles,
　　that you may bring salvation to the uttermost
　　parts of the earth.' "
And when the Gentiles heard this, they were glad
and glorified the word of God; and as many as were
ordained to eternal life believed (Acts 13:42-48).

Jesus had said to his disciples, "If they have received
me, they will receive you; and if they have rejected me,
they will reject you." Everywhere Paul went he found
this to be true. The gospel is like a knife cutting its way
through society, through men's hearts. It awakens, it hits
with impact, and it divides—men have to decide one way
or the other. Some decide for, some against. Some want
God and cry out to him, and are relieved and delivered;
others refuse, turn away, harden their hearts, and destroy themselves. This is what we see here. Certain Jews
and devout converts, i.e., Gentile converts to Judaism,
followed Paul and Barnabas, who spoke to them and
urged them to continue in the grace of God.

But there were also those who were filled with
jealousy and hostility, who contradicted and reviled, and
to them Paul proves, from the Scriptures, that the Scriptures authorize them to turn from the Jews and go to the

Gentiles if the Jews refuse this message. He quotes Isaiah:

> I have set you to be a light for the Gentiles, that you may bring salvation to the uttermost parts of the earth.

Then we are told:

> And when the Gentiles heard this, they were glad and glorified the word of God; and as many as were ordained to eternal life believed.

Now do not turn this around. The verse does not say, "And as many as believed were ordained to eternal life." Paul began this message by showing them that God is active, trying to reach out to men; it is not men who are trying to find God. When men believe, they are simply responding to the activity of God, who is already reaching out to them. Here were many who were ordained of God, and when they were thus ordained, they believed, they responded to God. You can never get away from this wonderful, mysterious combination of divine sovereignty and human responsibility.

This, by the way, is the same word that Paul uses in Romans 13 when he says, "The powers that be are ordained of God." In an election year we vote for men to be our governmental officials. Certain men, by their human will, decide to run for office. Others decide to vote for them; the people put them into office. Yet the Scripture says it is God who puts them there. I don't know how it works. God doesn't cancel out human responsibility, but underneath and above and all around is the sovereignty of God, working his wonderful purposes in human life.

The final result of Paul's sermon is given in the closing verses:

And the word of the Lord spread throughout all the region. But the Jews incited the devout women of high standing and the leading men of the city, and stirred up persecution against Paul and Barnabas, and drove them out of their district. But they shook off the dust from their feet against them, and went to Iconium. And the disciples were filled with joy and with the Holy Spirit (Acts 13:49-52).

Paul and Barnabas were evidently at Antioch for an extended time, probably several weeks, during which the Word of God went out into all the region around. But many of the Jews were disturbed by this and, as they could not prevail openly, they went around behind the scenes and stirred up a Women's Liberation Front. They went to devout women of high standing and through them they reached the Roman authorities (the leading men of the city) and thus drove them out of their district.

Dr. Luke, with his ability to deliver quick, precise summaries, does not give us all the details. Paul tells us that there were three times in his life when he was beaten by rods, an official action of the Romans. Once was later in Philippi, and many scholars feel that here was another occasion. Paul and Barnabas may have been brought before the Roman authorities and beaten with rods and thus driven out of the district. In any event, they shook off the dust of their feet against them and went to Iconium.

The last sentence is beautiful. The disciples who remained in this area were filled with joy and with the

Holy Spirit. There is no mention of the gift of tongues in connection with the filling of the Holy Spirit, but there is mention of the fruit of the Spirit. They were filled with the joy of the Lord and the love of God. This is the great sign of the Spirit of God in the human heart—it floods the heart with love and joy. If we are Christians our hearts cannot help but be moved at the mercy of God toward us, who deserve nothing at his hands. Yet how much he has given!

> **Our heavenly Father, our hearts are stirred as we think again of the mercy that you show to us, this marvelous justification by which all that has lain heavily on our hearts and our consciences has been washed away in the blood of Jesus Christ our Lord. And his life is given to us so that by it we may live on a totally different basis than we ever lived before. How wonderful this is, Lord! Teach us never to forget that we have been justified, and that whenever we fail or falter, your justification is there again, ready to wash us and cleanse us, to free us and restore us. In his name we thank you, Amen.**

CHAPTER THREE

COUNTERATTACK

Acts 14:1-28

In Acts 14 we will see Paul and Barnabas ministering in three different cities—Iconium, Lystra, and Derbe. In two of these cities they met with vicious and violent opposition. It is important for us to see how they handled this, because it is very likely, in the days to come, that many of us will face the same kind of conditions— violence and physical opposition, threatening us because of our faith.

Immediate Impact

We begin with the first verse of Chapter 14, as Paul and Barnabas come to the city of Iconium:

Now at Iconium they entered together into the Jewish synagogue, and so spoke that a great company believed, both of Jews and of Greeks. But the unbelieving Jews stirred up the Gentiles and poisoned their minds against the brethren. So they remained for a long time, speaking boldly for the Lord, who bore witness to the word of his grace, granting signs and wonders to be done by their hands. But the people of the city were divided; some

sided with the Jews, and some with the apostles (Acts 14:1-4).

Iconium, although a pagan Gentile city, had a strong colony of Jews who had a synagogue. As usual, Paul and Barnabas went there first, and their preaching had an impact. We read that they "so spoke that a great company believed, both of Jews and of Greeks." This was no bland, meaningless gospel; it was a gospel that hit like a ton of bricks. It shook people and jolted them and made them sit up and take notice. Immediately a great crowd believed when they heard Paul and Barnabas.

Since this was a synagogue it was a place where religious people had long gathered, going over the truth about God. A great deal of truth was available to them there, but their hearts were empty. All their knowledge had not brought them to peace and forgiveness and all the other great things for which they were searching the Scriptures. But when Paul and Barnabas declared the grace of God in Jesus, these people believed, and it made a tremendous change! It doesn't make any difference what your background has been—how dark or wrong, how smug or self-righteous or hypocritical. The great word of the gospel is that Jesus Christ cleanses, sets free, fills with adequacy, and makes men able to be what God intended them to be.

Subtle Opposition

A further effect of a genuine gospel message is that it will arouse opposition. We read, "But the unbelieving Jews stirred up the Gentiles and poisoned their minds against the brethren" (v. 2). In any Jewish synagogue there were many Gentiles trying to learn the truth about God. Luke says that certain of the Jews were un-believing. Literally, the word is "unpersuadable." They not only disbelieved the gospel but would not give it a chance or even consider it. These people stirred up the Gentiles who were present and poisoned their minds against the brethren.

Just how they did this we are not told. There is a very interesting account in the New Testament Apocrypha (certain books circulated in the early days with the claim that they were a part of Scripture, but which were never accepted as such). Among them is a book called "The Acts of Paul and Thecla," the setting of which is Iconium. According to this story the Apostle Paul fell in love with a young woman called Thecla, and their romance became so torrid that it broke up her whole family and thus turned the city against them. I am sure this was not an actual event. The book is dated probably two centuries or so after Paul lived. But it does perhaps reflect something of the methods these Jews used to poison the minds of the Gentiles, by suggesting that the gospel being preached would destroy a family relationship.

At any rate, the apostles ran into subtle opposition. No one knows exactly how the enemy is going to strike back. Paul says, "We are not ignorant of his devices"; that is, we know what schemes the devil uses against us. The devil has a limited bag of tricks from which he can operate. But what we do not know is which one of them he is going to employ on any given occasion. There is an element of surprise in the devil's work, and here is a clear case in point. These men were not met with the outright, open opposition they faced in Antioch, but with subtle, whispering, deceitful, poisonous propaganda, turning many people away from the truth. Luke, with characteristic brevity, does not give us all the details, but it is evident that the apostles somehow overcame this opposition, for we read,

So they remained for a long time, speaking boldly for the Lord, who bore witness to the word of his grace, granting signs and wonders to be done by their hands (Acts 14:3).

They were probably there for several months, possibly as long as six months. During this time, despite the subtle propaganda against the gospel, a sweeping proclamation of the truth went forward. Many were turning to Christ, and God worked with his apostles, confirming the Word with signs and wonders.

Supernatural Evidence

Here is another significant element which is always present when the true gospel is being preached. There is a baffling quality about it; things happen which are beyond the ability of men to bring about. It is the supernatural evidence of the truth of the gospel which makes it so attractive and compelling to the world. This strange confirmation does not always involve physical miracles, although it did in those days, and it does in certain places again today. But these physical miracles are simply parables for us of the spiritual freedom that God intends to give. The character of the miracles occurring today is primarily that men and women are set free to be what they never could have been without Jesus Christ. Some of them struggle for years to free themselves from habits, thoughts, and attitudes that are harmful and injurious to them, but without success. When they come to Christ, however, he strikes off the shackles, and they are free.

That baffling supernatural element must be present in every single Christian. If there is not that quality about you as a Christian which cannot be explained in terms of your personality, or your background or education, or your heredity, then you really have nothing more to offer to your neighbors and friends than any other person would have. There must be that mysterious element which makes people scratch their heads and say, "I don't understand him (or her). His attitude and reactions are unaccountable. I don't understand his ability to show love. It's something quite different from what I'm used to." That is God at work.

The Sword of Division

The last mark of the gospel given in this section is that of division:

> **But the people of the city were divided; some sided with the Jews, and some with the apostles (Acts 14:4).**

The gospel is like a ferment turned loose in society. It is not intended to bring peace, except to the individual heart; it is intended to be divisive. Jesus said, "Do you think I have come to bring peace on earth? No. I have come to bring a sword." He certainly did not mean the sword of warfare and physical violence. He made that very clear. He meant that the message he proclaimed was intended to divide men. One of the marks of true evangelism is always that those who are being affected by it are divided. They are either for it or against it. No neutrality is possible when the gospel is preached in the power of the Holy Spirit. If there is a church in a city and that city is not divided, then there is something wrong with the church, because it is not preaching the gospel as it ought to be preached. There ought to be a clear-cut division among people as the gospel comes in.

Before we move on, notice one other interesting thing here. For the first time in the Book of Acts both Barnabas and Paul are called apostles (in verses 4 and 14), showing that other men besides the twelve and Paul were called apostles.

Eventually the animosity of the apostles' opponents intensified dangerously. But, as usual, this by no means prevented a wider preaching of the gospel.

When an attempt was made by both Gentiles and Jews, with their rulers, to molest them and to stone them, they learned of it and fled to Lystra and Derbe, cities of Lycaonia, and to the surrounding country; and there they preached the gospel (Acts 14:5-7).

Thus we come to the second city in this chapter, the Gentile city of Lystra, where there was no Jewish synagogue. With no obvious place to begin, what will they do now? Let's see what happens:

Now at Lystra there was a man sitting, who could not use his feet; he was a cripple from birth, who had never walked. He listened to Paul speaking; and Paul, looking intently at him and seeing that he had faith to be made well, said in a loud voice, "Stand upright on your feet." And he sprang up and walked.

And when the crowds saw what Paul had done, they lifted up their voices, saying in Lycaonian, "The gods have come down to us in the likeness of men!" Barnabas they called Zeus, and Paul, because he was the chief speaker, they called Hermes. And the priest of Zeus, whose temple was in front of the city, brought oxen and garlands to the gates and wanted to offer sacrifice with the people (Acts 14:8-13).

When Paul and Barnabas came into this city they had no idea what they were going to do. They didn't form a committee and say, "Well, let's see if we can get the Chamber of Commerce report on the city's population distribution. Then we could divide it into squares and evangelize in a systematic way." They had no plans other than to be there and to do what God sent them to do—to preach. So they walked right into the marketplace and began, trusting the Lord to have prepared certain people, to have men of his choosing ready to open the door to the city.

As they proclaimed the gospel, God began to work in an amazing way. Sitting in the marketplace was a man who had been lame from his birth, who had never walked. He was evidently well-known throughout the city, having been there all his life. As Paul preached, probably for several days in a row, this man listened and believed what Paul was declaring about the power of Jesus, the mighty Son of God. One day Paul looked at him and saw in that man's eyes the faith to believe. Suddenly, unquestionably led of the Spirit, he said to him, "Stand upright on your feet." And the lame man, though he had never walked in his life, made the effort to obey. He had faith enough to try, and the moment he began to obey, the power to obey was given.

The Christian life always works that way. It doesn't make any difference whether the problem is physical, emotional, or spiritual; you are going to be held in its bondage until you begin to obey the Word of God about it. When you make the effort to obey, God will set you free. But he will never move until you obey. That's the way faith works. Most people are kept from seeing God at work in their lives because they keep waiting for God to do something in order for them to believe. But God has already done all that he is going to do, and when you believe what he says, then he will give you the power to be free.

This miracle is a mighty parable of the many people who have been spiritually lame, unable to take a step toward God, but who have been set free to do so by the gospel. This miracle cracked the city wide open. The whole populace immediately took note of Paul and Barnabas in their midst. Ordinarily the city would not have been open to the preaching of the gospel, and God's full purpose would not have been accomplished there.

Appeal to the Ego

But the enemy was also at work. Without wasting a moment, he managed to pervert the situation so that these people would not hear the word. He twisted and distorted the people's perception just enough to lay the groundwork for a further attack against the apostles. We are told that these superstitious, pagan people cried out, "Why, the gods have come down to us!" The Greek names they gave the apostles were Zeus and Hermes; the Roman names were Jupiter and Mercury. Perhaps because Barnabas had a long beard and dignified bearing they called him Jupiter, or Zeus. Because Paul was small and talked a lot he was called Mercury, or Hermes, the spokesman for the gods. What a subtle attack! Here was an appeal to the ego of the apostles. Imagine going into a strange city and being welcomed as gods!

On a recent trip to Hawaii I visited the wax museum in Honolulu and saw the diorama depicting the landing of Captain James Cook of the British Navy on the shores of Hawaii, at Kealakekua Bay. He was welcomed as the god Lono, and he and his men were given anything and everything they wanted. They were attended to day and night. But one day as they were about to launch their boats and return to their ship, a native who was angry with Captain Cook for some reason grabbed hold of him, forgetting that he was supposedly a god. Captain Cook swung at him and knocked him down. The native retaliated, hitting him on the head with a club, and the captain groaned. When the natives heard this, one of them cried out, "He groans. He is not a god!" and they fell on him and killed him. You can see a memorial at the site today. In Lystra, these apostles had a perfect opportunity to take over the city on their own terms! What a subtle attack this flattery was. Sometimes popularity is the weapon Satan employs most successfully to ruin the presentation of the gospel. But notice how Paul and Barnabas receive it:

> **But when the apostles Barnabas and Paul heard of it [they didn't understand the native speech of these people, even though Paul had the gift of tongues. The gift is not intended for preaching the gospel nor understanding another language, so someone had to tell them what was happening], they tore their garments and rushed out among the multitude, crying,**

"Men, why are you doing this? We also are men, of like nature with you, and bring you good news, that you should turn from these vain things to a living God who made the heaven and the earth and the sea and all that is in them. In past generations he allowed all the nations to walk in their own ways; yet he did not leave himself without witness, for he did good and gave you from heaven rains and fruitful seasons, satisfying your hearts with food and gladness." With these words they scarcely restrained the people from offering sacrifice to them (Acts 14:14-18).

If you want to know how to reach your neighbors who are not interested in the gospel and who know nothing of Scripture, who have not been to church and are not interested in it, the approach to take is through nature. When Paul went to the Jews, he started with the Scriptures, the truth of God that they already knew. When he went to the Gentiles, he started with nature, the truth of God which *they* already knew.

Paul points out three things that would have been very plain to his hearers if they had been thinking about their contact with nature. First he shows that behind creation there is one living God, not a multitude of relatively powerless, desperate, and divided pagan deities or idols. If Paul's hearers had really observed nature, they would have realized that it is not controlled by a conglomerate of separate powers, all trying to compete with one another, as envisioned in the pagan pantheon. According to the pagan system, everything had a god. There was a god of water, a god of trees, a god of rocks. Even the processes of the body had gods: there was a god for speech, a god for sex, and a god for life. These gods, like people, were in competition with one another. Paul is saying, "You haven't really seen nature. You haven't noticed, obviously, that nature is as one; it all ties together because it has been made by one God, who is a living God. It is sustained and held together in harmony, and is constantly being renewed. So there is one living God." Paul declares to them in no uncertain terms that nature has borne witness to God.

The second point he makes is that the one living God permits men free choice, and therefore allows evil. The problem of evil among men forms the basis of constant arguments from humanists and others, who say, "If your God is such a loving God, why does he permit suffering? Why does he allow evil, and injustice, and war?" These pagans were quite aware of these arguments. They understood them and argued the same way as such people do today. Paul answers by saying, "What you must know is that God, in generations past, allowed all the nations to walk in their own way." In other words, he gave them free will. In order to permit free will, he must allow evil. That is Paul's argument, and it is unanswerable.

There are those today who say, "Why doesn't God stop all the wars and injustices?" Well, he could. But if he did, he would take away your freedom of choice, and that is the one thing you don't want to surrender. The greatest dignity of humanity is the power to choose between two possible routes. God has given us that power, and he will not take it away. Paul says that this is the reason God allows evil.

But third, he says, God will not allow evil to go too far. He does not allow evil to engulf humanity and wipe us off the face of the earth, as human evil would surely do in a few months' time if it were unrestrained. God has restrained it. And right in the midst of it, despite all the rejection and rebellion and blasphemy and hatred that is poured out against him by these people whom he loves, God has shown his love by giving rain and fruit and harvest and gladness in the family circle and joy and happiness throughout the various moments of life. That is the God whom Paul preached. What a marvelous declaration of the gospel, that God had given all these things and thus had given witness to these people about himself!

The Marks of Jesus

So the first onslaught of the enemy falls back upon itself. The city is open to the gospel, and Paul is able to proclaim it in power. But soon the devil's evil comes full cycle. Look at the next event:

> **But Jews came there from Antioch and Iconium; and having persuaded the people, they stoned Paul and dragged him out of the city, supposing that he was dead. But when the disciples gathered about him, he rose up and entered the city; and on the next day he went on with Barnabas to Derbe (Acts 14:19, 20).**

Here is the counterattack of the enemy again, striking back to hinder the gospel as soon as its power is unleashed. This time he falls back on his old reliable — violence. His spadework has created a climate in which the people can be persuaded to condone the stoning of the person who would be their benefactor. This is the only time that Paul was stoned—not with drugs, but with hard, sharp rocks which cut his body, bruised and crushed him, and left him lying in a crumpled heap on the pavement. His enemies dragged him outside the city gates and threw him on the rubbish dump, thinking he was dead. You can imagine Barnabas and the disciples gathered around him there, weeping over this beloved, faithful preacher whom they too thought to be dead.

This may well be the time when Paul received those marks in his body to which he refers later in his Letter to the Galatians. The church in Lystra was one of the Galatian churches. Paul writes, "I bear on my body the marks of Jesus" (Gal. 6:17). He may have received those marks when he was stoned at Lystra. In any case, as his friends are gathered around him, weeping and lamenting his death, perhaps speaking of burial, the apostle suddenly sits up and says, "Hold the undertaker! You're not going to bury Paul yet." And God restores him. Was he dead? This is a question many ask, but Luke says no, he was not dead. "*Supposing* him to be dead, they dragged him out of the city." Luke can surely be trusted in this judgment. As he journeyed with Paul later he certainly must have questioned him closely about this event. As a doctor, his medical interest would have been aroused, and he was satisfied that Paul had not died. But Paul was miraculously restored, and the next day he went on to Derbe.

So far we have seen the pattern of approach to the religious crowd as well as the pattern of approach to the pagan crowd. We have seen how to handle the various attacks of Satan by faithful obedience to the commission which God has given. In the last part of the chapter we learn about another important feature which is basic to the gospel—body life:

When they had preached the gospel to that city [Derbe] and had made many disciples, they returned to Lystra and to Iconium and to Antioch, strengthen-

ing the souls of the disciples, exhorting them to continue in the faith, and saying that through many
tribulations we must enter the kingdom of God. And
when they had appointed elders for them in every
church, with prayer and fasting, they committed
them to the Lord in whom they believed (Acts 14:21-
23).

What tremendous evidence of courage! They had
been expelled from Antioch of Pisidia, threatened in
Iconium, and actually stoned in Lystra, but when God
raises Paul up they go right back into those same cities to
strengthen the disciples. This kind of courage comes only
from trust in the living God; they were confident that
God was going with them. It was essential to the life of
the church that they gather the disciples together and
minister to them. The Christian life is more than merely
being converted; it is growing in Christ. It is going on to
be what God intended you to be in Christ, which involves certain provisions.

Provisions for Growth

Notice three important things the apostles did. First,
they taught the disciples. "They strengthened the souls
of the disciples." You do that by teaching the Word of
God. The Word is what sets men free, but people must
know the truth before they can be set free. So they
taught them by expounding the Word to them. Second,
they exhorted them to continue in the faith. This is
usually done by an appeal to example. They went back
over the Old Testament record and pointed out how men
and women of God had been living by faith for years,

and how God had blessed and strengthened them. The eleventh chapter of Hebrews is a mighty testimony of this sort. Third, they enlightened these new believers as to the meaning of tribulation. They said, "You're going to go through trouble, but don't be surprised. This is what will make a real, genuine man or woman out of you. It will make you grow. You need tribulation, so thank God for it." In this way they taught them how to view hardship.

Not only did they teach the new disciples, but they also recognized the spiritual gifts that were present. They noted that the Holy Spirit had equipped men and women for ministry in the church, and they appointed elders in every church, with prayer and fasting.

Finally, they prayed and committed the people to the Lord. Thus, as they moved on, the church was able to grow and expand and preach throughout the whole area (as we will see when the apostles come back later) because they were solidly grounded. At last they were able to return to the church at Antioch, from which they had been sent out:

> Then they passed through Pisidia, and came to Pamphylia. And when they had spoken the word in Perga, they went down to Attalia; and from there they sailed to Antioch, where they had been commended to the grace of God for the work which they had fulfilled. And when they arrived, they gathered the church together and declared all that God had done with them, and how he had opened a door of faith to the Gentiles. And they remained no little time with the disciples (Acts 14:24-28).

This was a missionary meeting, with a report of what has happened, much as churches have in our time.

Missionaries come to us periodically to tell us what is going on in the far reaches of the world as the gospel is penetrating in power there today. What an exciting time it must have been for the people gathered together to hear the apostles speak, as they saw the scars on Paul's body and heard the marvelous stories of the thousands who had come to Christ through the ministry of these faithful men! By trusting God they had been able to turn back all the attacks of the enemy and could therefore encourage the home church by their experience of God's faithfulness and power in the midst of opposition.

Our Father, we ask you to make us faithful followers of these mighty apostles, our brethren of the early centuries. Like them, Lord, help us to trust in a living God who is changing men's hearts and delivering their minds from the grip and power of the evil one. Help us to rejoice as we too see the power of the Word of God in our own day. We ask in your name, Amen.

CHAPTER FOUR

CAUSE FOR ALARM

Acts 15:1-21

Paul and Barnabas and the other believers who proclaimed the truth of God in the first century met with bitter and violent opposition everywhere they went, as we have just seen. Riots were created in cities where they preached, and everywhere they preached they were confronted with such heavy opposition that their lives were threatened. But the tactics of the enemy are not limited to external opposition; these men also met with treacherous betrayal from within.

In the fifteenth chapter of Acts we have the story of the worst of these inner betrayals of the gospel, the emergence of what we can only call false Christianity. You will never understand Christianity or the church until you understand that there are always present, in any so-called Christian gathering, manifestations and representatives of both true and false Christianity. Unfortunately, false Christianity is believed by millions who think they have understood the truth. Therefore their minds are closed to the truth when it comes. The characteristics of this kind of false Christianity, which is unthinkingly accepted by millions of people today as the real thing, are described in this chapter. Luke gives us the background in the opening verses:

> But some men came down from Judea [to Antioch] and were teaching the brethren, "Unless you are circumcised according to the custom of Moses, you cannot be saved." And when Paul and Barnabas had no small dissension and debate with them, Paul and Barnabas and some of the others were appointed to go up to Jerusalem to the apostles and the elders about this question (Acts 15:1, 2).

Here is another greatly condensed account of events which actually occurred over a period of several months. It all began with the introduction of a very plausible and attractive heresy which came disguised as Christianity. Luke says that certain Jewish brethren, who were ostensibly Christians, came down from Jerusalem to Antioch. They came among the Gentile believers there, who had been, until just recently, devotees of the licentious and sexually immoral practices of the pagan temples. These Gentiles had been hopeless in their outlook toward the future beyond this life and were sunken in despair and darkness. But God had saved them, and they were now rejoicing in Christ.

But these Jewish brethren came to them and said, "Unless you are circumcised according to the custom of Moses, you cannot be saved." This introduced an issue which split the church at Antioch wide open. They were really saying, "In order to become a Christian, you must first become a Jew. Unless you become a Jew you are a second-class Christian, if a Christian at all." Thus they challenged the gospel of the grace of God as Paul and Barnabas had been proclaiming it.

Race and Ritual

The first really serious internal strife within the church was over race and ritual—over the question of Jews versus Gentiles, and of circumcision as the sign of acceptance. This specific issue has long ago passed away as a concern to us, but the principle behind it is very definitely still present today. The enemy has simply changed the players on the program, substituting new issues on the same old divisive platform.

In many places today the issue is whether blacks are supposed to worship with whites. One of the largest churches in Birmingham, Alabama, was split for weeks over the question of whether they ought to admit one lone black woman to membership in a church which had never had a black member for 98 years!

More widely, this same principle is involved in the feelings of many Christians toward any group or individual who is different from them in some way. At the height of the hippie movement one young man was working successfully within the hippie culture in Los Angeles, bringing great crowds of them into the church he represented. He was finally dismissed because, as the official board of that church put it, "He's bringing the riffraff off the streets into the church." That is the kind of issue they had in Antioch.

I remember how shocked I was a few years ago at the reply a young couple gave to my suggestion that they visit another couple who were newcomers to our church. They looked at me and said, "Oh, no, you don't want them. They're not our kind of people." It was all I could do to restrain myself from tongue-lashing them on the spot, because that is a hateful denial of the universality of the church and of its inclusion of all types and ages and backgrounds and races.

Rituals, as well as people, often become bones of contention today. Substitute baptism for circumcision and you bring the issue right up to date. Some people insist that unless you undergo the ritual of a haircut, you cannot become a Christian. Barbers have become the priests of our day! Others say that no one should be admitted to a church gathering unless he has his shoes on. But I have searched the Scriptures and cannot find anything there which says you must wear shoes to church. These external issues are the kinds of things that are splitting Christians apart today, even as the issue of circumcision was in Antioch.

This issue had great power over these new Christians. They were relatively untaught, and the whole idea appeared very plausible on several grounds. First of all, these men who came down from Jerusalem were evidently sincere. They were not simply trying to cause trouble; they were deeply committed to the belief that unless a Gentile complied with the law of Moses and was circumcised, he had no right to call himself a Christian. This whole concept struck with such tremendous force because of the sincerity of these men.

Furthermore, the issue appeared to have a great deal of Scriptural support. There are passages in the Old Testament which say that ultimately Israel will rule over the Gentile nations, and that the Jews are chosen as God's own people, with a peculiarly special relationship to him. These men went through the Scriptures and selected these verses, ignoring others that temper and balance them, and, like any good cultist today, they presented a tremendously appealing program that seemed to be based solidly in Scripture. With it they shook the faith of these people in Antioch.

What they were doing was failing to allow God to

reveal new truth. They were basing their position on the assumption that all truth had already been given in that day. But the Scriptures were not yet completed; God *was* revealing new truth. Remember that the Apostle Paul tells us very plainly that this whole truth about the Jews and the Gentiles becoming one body in Jesus Christ was never mentioned in the Old Testament. He says it was a mystery hidden from previous generations until it was revealed to the apostles and the prophets of the New Testament era. But for this reason it was difficult indeed to prove that receiving uncircumcized believers into the church was not a violation of the Scriptures.

Third, the position of these men appeared to be supported by the church in Jerusalem. The views came from James, the brother of our Lord Jesus himself, who had been raised with Jesus and could testify to the fact that Jesus obeyed the law and was circumcised according to the law of Moses. By using these arguments they had great power in the preaching of this heresy. Thus it is no wonder that Luke says, in a characteristic understatement, that they caused no small dissension and debate!

Though we are not told so here, this is unquestionably the time when that incident occurred which the Apostle Paul records in his Letter to the Galatians. The Apostle Peter had come down to Antioch and at first had perfect freedom to eat with the Gentiles. Peter enjoyed his first taste of a ham sandwich, and he had bacon and eggs every morning. He was rejoicing in his freedom in Christ. But, Paul says, when certain men came down from James and began to preach that you cannot be saved unless you are circumcised according to the law of Moses, Peter (think of it—Peter the Apostle!) was carried away by this dissension. He went over to the kosher table for breakfast and no longer ate with the Gentiles. And Barnabas (Barnabas, Paul's faithful colaborer in the dissemination of the gospel!) was likewise carried away briefly, until Paul straightened him out. Paul had to rebuke the Apostle Peter publicly for his inconsistency. You can see what Luke means when he says this was no small debate. This was an issue which threatened to divide Christianity for the rest of the time!

The church appointed Paul and Barnabas to go up to Jerusalem. Be careful not to read this as though Paul was uncertain as to the truth and had to consult with the other apostles before it was settled. Paul never had a moment's doubt over this issue. He tells us in Galatians that he went to Jerusalem by revelation; the Lord told him to go. Paul was prepared to defy all twelve apostles and the whole church of Jerusalem if they should differ with him on this issue, because he knew what the Lord Jesus had revealed to him directly. He did not get his gospel from the apostles; he got it from the Lord. So he stood firm. For a while the whole fate of the gospel hung upon this one man's faithfulness.

First Ecumenical Council

Paul went to Jerusalem because this was the best way to silence these Judaizing teachers. If the church at Jerusalem would repudiate this doctrine, then the Judaisers would be thwarted and their teaching would be discredited. Luke takes us to this first ecumenical council:

When they came to Jerusalem, they were welcomed by the church and the apostles and the elders, and

they declared all that God had done with them. But some believers who belonged to the party of the Pharisees rose up, and said, "It is necessary to circumcise them, and to charge them to keep the law of Moses."

The apostles and the elders were gathered together to consider this matter. And after there had been much debate, Peter rose and said to them, "Brethren, you know that in the early days God made choice among you, that by my mouth the Gentiles should hear the word of the gospel and believe. And God who knows the heart bore witness to them, giving them the Holy Spirit just as he did to us; and he made no distinction between us and them, but cleansed their hearts by faith. Now therefore why do you make trial of God by putting a yoke upon the neck of the disciples which neither our fathers nor we have been able to bear? But we believe that we shall be saved through the grace of the Lord Jesus, just as they will."

And all the assembly kept silence; and they listened to Barnabas and Paul as they related what signs and wonders God had done through them among the Gentiles (Acts 15:4-12).

From this account alone it would seem as though only one great meeting took place in Jerusalem, but actually there were three. First there was a body-life service when Paul and Barnabas arrived. This was the first time these men had appeared in Jerusalem after their triumphant missionary journey through the Galatian cities, and so they were welcomed home. What a grand occasion it must have been as Paul and Barnabas stood up and told about all that God had done! They told of how they had held street meetings in front of saloons in the various cities where they went, of how riots had started over them, of how they had been kicked out of assemblies and driven out of towns. They told of how God had worked with them through it all, confirming their words and changing the lives of many. The whole church in Jerusalem was stirred as they heard this account.

The next day there was a private meeting which Paul mentions in Galatians 2, but which Luke does not record here. There Paul and the other apostles and the elders sat down and together discussed Paul's theology. "At the end of that meeting," Paul says, "It was quite apparent that these men who had lived and traveled with the Lord Jesus had absolutely nothing to add to me." In other words, Paul had learned from the Lord directly what Jesus had taught the others through the whole scope of his ministry. Paul's gospel was exactly the same as theirs. "And when they saw that," Paul says, "they extended to me the right hand of fellowship and put their blessing upon my ministry. We realized that we were proclaiming exactly the same truth."

Focus on Titus

On the next day was the great general meeting in which the leaders took up this very divisive issue of whether a person had to be circumcised in order to be a Christian. Titus had come to Jerusalem with Paul on this occasion, and he now became the focus of contention. The question was whether this young man, who was a Greek and not a Jew, had to be circumcised or not. You can imagine how embarrassed poor Titus was, but Paul tells us in Galatians that this was the issue. There was a great deal of debate, as Luke records; there always is in such a meeting. The issue must be thoroughly aired, and there are always two kinds of speakers: those who have something to say, and those who have to say something. So it went on and on.

Finally Peter stood up. It is important to note that Peter did not convene this council. If, as our Catholic friends tell us, he had been the first pope, that would have been his responsibility. But he did not. James was the president of the council and Peter was merely a spokesman. Notice also that they did not settle anything by majority vote. They were seeking the mind of the Spirit, which would be expressed in a sense of unity that they would all recognize. That is why the issues had to be clearly aired.

Actually, I'm surprised that Peter kept silent as long as he did; he was always opening his mouth to change feet. But he was probably chastened and humbled by the recent rebuke he had received from the Apostle Paul, and so, biding his time and awaiting God's moment, he finally rose to speak. He had three things to say: first he reminded the leaders that at the very beginning of his ministry God had taught him a great lesson along this line, stripping him of all the ugly Jewish prejudices he had retained even as a Christian. God made him face up to the fact that he loved and searched for and wanted non-Jewish believers as much as Jews. Peter had told, in an earlier council in Jerusalem, of the struggle he went through in this area. Now he reminds them again of how, in the home of Cornelius, he had learned something new about the heart of God.

Then (and this is very significant, coming from a Jew) he admits to them publicly and openly—challenging them to deny it—that the effort to obey the law by trying their hardest was nothing but a burdensome yoke upon their necks, and that it always had been such a yoke, throughout Jewish history:

Now therefore why do you make trial of God by putting a yoke upon the neck of the disciples which neither our fathers nor we have been able to bear (Acts 15:10)?

Nobody ever came to God by trying to be good or by religious ritual. Never. No Jew, no Gentile, no one ever came to him that way. In the effort to do so, people have only been bowed down under such an intolerable weight that they have often been crushed in despair.

Peter's third point is a real blockbuster. He says to these Jews, "Look, I believe that we Jews will be saved through the grace of the Lord Jesus, just as those Gentiles will." Notice that Peter does not say, "*They* will be saved, just as *we* will," as might be expected. In other words, the norm for God's operation in saving men is *more visible* when he saves a Gentile than it is when he saves a Jew. The Jew often confuses the issue by his efforts at self-righteousness. But the Gentile does not try that. He usually accepts the grace of God because he has no other place to turn. So Peter says, "I have come to see that we Jews are on exactly the same basis as these Gentiles, when it comes to being saved."

This thought-provoking statement had the impressive effect of bringing silence to the whole assembly. Even the Judaizers were stunned by this argument. They all stopped talking and started thinking. Then they listened as Barnabas and Paul related what signs and wonders God had done through them among the Gentiles. Paul and Barnabas seized the occasion to confirm the words of Peter by showing that God was doing the very thing he said, not only in saving men but also in confirming that these two men were apostles. They had the signs of an apostle to prove it, the signs and wonders that God had done through them. (This is probably when Paul and Barnabas received the right hand of fellowship, acknowledging that they were indeed authenticated apostles.)

At this point James, the chairman of the meeting, speaks, and this is the conclusion of the whole event:

> After they finished speaking, James replied, "Brethren, listen to me. Symeon [i.e., Peter] has related how God first visited the Gentiles, to take out of them a people for his name. And with this the words of the prophets agree, as it is written,
> 'After this I will return,
>   and I will rebuild the dwelling of David,
>   which has fallen;
> I will rebuild its ruins,
>   and I will set it up,
> that the rest of men may seek the Lord,
>   and all the Gentiles who are called by my name,
>   says the Lord, who has made these things
>   known from of old.'
> Therefore my judgment is that we should not trouble those of the Gentiles who turn to God, but should write to them to abstain from the pollutions of idols and from unchastity [literally, fornication] and from what is strangled and from blood. For from early generations Moses has had in every city those who preach him, for he is read every sabbath in the synagogues" (Acts 15:13-21).

This is an extremely important statement. It is made by the man who was the flesh-and-blood brother of the

Lord Jesus. He had been raised in that home in Nazareth and had seen all that his older Brother had done all his life. He had not believed in him until after the resurrection, but in the resurrection he saw confirmation of all the witness that the Spirit had borne to his heart through those years, and he became a believer in Jesus Christ. He holds the utmost respect from all factions in the church. He is called "James the Just" and "Old Camel-knees" because he prayed so long he wore holes in his robe and raised calluses on his knees. He is a man of tremendous integrity.

He summarizes now, after listening to the mind of the Spirit. He says four things which are of extreme importance. First, he comes squarely to terms with the activity of God. These Judaizers had been saying to the Gentiles, "Without circumcision you cannot be saved." But they were ignoring one very stubborn fact: these Gentiles were *already* saved. God had already been saving Gentiles without asking anybody's permission to do so, and he was doing it without any ritual, or even any reference to the law of Moses. And with this point they could not argue. This was extremely important because it forced them to take note of the direction of God's activity. They saw that God was already doing what they said could not be done, and thus God was overruling them.

Be Sure It Is God

But now notice the second point. It is supremely important! The activity was accepted as the valid activity of God only as it corresponded to the written Word of God. I wish I could get this point across to people today. There

is so much activity going on in our day which is being
called the work of the Spirit of God, but which is not in
line with what the Word of God says. And people are
accepting it naively, ingenuously, because it has some
appearance of supernatural activity. It is all right to note
what God is doing, but we must be sure it is *God* who is
doing it. Whatever does not correspond with the Word of
God is not the activity of God, no matter how good it may
look.

There is so much occurring like this today. There are
meetings where people break out into tongues, and
everyone says, "Oh, look at the restoration of the gift of
tongues. God is at work. The Spirit is at work!" My
question is, "Is it the Biblical gift of tongues?" When you
compare it with what the Bible says about the gift of
tongues, there is scarcely any resemblance at all. So I
must say, "That is not God at work." Another example is
healings. I certainly believe that God can heal; I am not
denying that. But each healing must be questioned in
order to discern where it comes from. James accepted
this activity among the Gentiles as from God because he
saw that it corresponded to the Word of God. He quoted
one of the prophets, Amos, who had predicted that there
would come a time when the Gentiles would be reached.
There are certain scholars today who attempt to imply
that James is giving here a sort of outline of future
events. "After this [the second coming] Jesus will return
and restore Israel, rebuild the dwelling of David . . . .
And then the Gentiles who are called by my name shall
come to Christ . . . ." But I honestly do not think he is
doing that. James views this prediction by Amos as
referring to the first coming of Jesus. I do not question
that there is a greater fulfillment awaiting us at the
second coming. But here he is talking about the first

coming, the coming of the Lord as the son of David to gather up all the crushed and broken hopes of the Davidic line and to fulfill the promise made to David by God: "Thou shalt never lack a king to set upon the throne . . . ." The fact is that the gospel, by that first coming, began to go out to the Gentiles. In other words, James is confirming by the prediction of the Word of God what Peter and Paul and Barnabas had declared. His point is that God intends to save Gentiles and has already begun in the home of Cornelius.

Third, James gives three or four very practical suggestions for a letter to the Gentile believers, suggestions designed to lay this controversy to rest. He says, "We should write to them to abstain from idolatry, from fornication [sexual immorality], from eating that which is strangled, and from eating blood. For from early generations Moses has in every city those who preach him [and who would therefore be offended]." Notice the classification here: two things in the moral realm (idolatry and sexual immorality) and two things in the realm of Christian love, of sensitivity and understanding toward others. If the Gentiles ate animals that were strangled, or if they ate blood, they would have great difficulty in fellowshipping with Jewish believers in Christ, who still clung to some of the dietary laws. So James wisely suggests that they should, in love, forego these practices in order to have fellowship in the body of Christ.

Denials of Faith

But notice that there is a footnote in the Revised Standard Version which suggests that the words "and from what is strangled" are not in the better texts (here and also in verse 29, later in the chapter). I personally believe that this phrase was not in the original text, and that James pointed out only three things: they were to abstain from idolatry, from fornication, and from blood, which in this context means murder. I feel that this is the case not only because of the manuscript support but also because these practices are direct denials of Christian faith in the areas of the spirit, the soul, and the body of man. If you do these things, James is saying, you are denying by your actions what you affirm is your faith.

The Scriptures support this reading. Paul says, "You cannot eat at the table of idols and the table of the Lord." In the Spirit, you can only worship one god. It is either God or a demon; one or the other. In the soul, you can only give your inner life to one lord. If you give it away in sexual immorality, you are destroying yourself. Interestingly, Scripture everywhere warns against this. Peter himself says, "Flee youthful passions, which war against the soul." In other words, sexual immorality—fornication—is the most devastating thing you can do to yourself psychologically. It destroys your emotional life. It breaks up the inner integrity of your humanity. This is why the Bible says that nations which give themselves to widespread immorality are bringing upon themselves sure destruction, because they are undermining the whole structure of society. And of course the third evil practice, against the body, is very evident. John says, "You know that no murderer has eternal life abiding in him." You cannot, as an individual, take the life of another person in anger and still claim that you really belong to Jesus Christ.

In the fourth point, the most important of all, James defines the supreme purpose of God today:

Peter has related how God first visited the Gentiles, to take out of them a people for his name.

Here is the focus of history: during the entire history of human life the one thing God is doing is calling out a people for his name. Everything that happens in history or current events relates somehow to this great program of God. God may permit terrible catastrophes and awful persecutions and judgments to come upon a people in order to make them wake up to reality and turn to him, so that he will be able to call out a people for his name. He may isolate a nation for years, perhaps centuries, in order to shut it off and allow it to sink into darkness and despair and hopelessness. Then, at the right psychological moment, he can open the door and let the gospel in, and the people will respond in great numbers. I believe that this is what God is doing in China today. Everything relates to this one great task of God.

According to the Bible, one of these days our great American cities are going to lie in ashes, crumbled to dust, destroyed, perhaps in a great nuclear holocaust (1 Pet. 3:7, 10). Civilization will be tremendously altered, with much of it destroyed. Out of the crumbling chaos of those days one institution involving humans will survive, and only one: the church of the Lord Jesus Christ, a people called out for his name's sake. Unless your life, and my life, finds a part in that program, it too is worthless.

Only what *God* does is worthwhile. And if we do not find a part in what God is doing, in reaching out to all the nations and all the cultures and the tribes and peoples of earth, to call out from among them a people for his name, we have no justification for having lived.

Our Father, help us to take these words with utmost

seriousness, as they were taken in the first century, so as to split the world wide open in that day. Help us to do the same in our own day, realizing that your great purpose has gone forward relentlessly. Throughout all the changing currents of human history, you are accomplishing what you set out to do. Grant that we may have a part, giving ourselves to the Lord Jesus, that we may be instruments of his working. We pray in his name, Amen.

CHAPTER FIVE

THE WAY GOD GUIDES
Acts 15:22—16:10

The most baffling and difficult problem with which young Christians often wrestle is how to determine the will of God. In the first chapter of this book, we began to see something of the strategy of the Holy Spirit. We saw that if we simply go about our business—that is, put into practice the truths we know, using the spiritual gifts we have been given—the Spirit will open up opportunities and guide us faithfully to do the will of God. That is his responsibility. In the section before us now, we have a further revelation on this vital matter—seven practical ways we can know God's will. The first way appears in the paragraph describing the conclusion of the great council at Jerusalem, where the early church settled the question of whether Gentiles needed to be circumcised in order to become Christians.

> Then it seemed good to the apostles and the elders, with the whole church, to choose men from among them and send them to Antioch with Paul and Barnabas. They sent Judas called Barsabbas, and Silas, leading men among the brethren, with the following letter: "The brethren, both the apostles and the elders, to the brethren who are of the Gentiles in An-

tioch and Syria and Cilicia, greeting. Since we have heard that some persons from us have troubled you with words, unsettling your minds, although we gave them no instructions, it has seemed good to us in assembly to choose men and send them to you with our beloved Barnabas and Paul, men who have risked their lives for the sake of our Lord Jesus Christ. We have therefore sent Judas and Silas, who themselves will tell you the same things by word of mouth. For it seemed good to the Holy Spirit and to us to lay upon you no greater burden than these necessary things: that you abstain from what has been sacrificed to idols and from blood and from what is strangled and from unchastity [or fornication]. If you keep yourselves from these, you will do well. Farewell" (Acts 15:22-29).

This is the way the council conveyed to the outlying churches the decision reached by the apostles and the elders. It is vital to see that this early church settled a question of doctrine by first hearing everybody's viewpoint. Everyone had a chance to say what he thought the Scriptures taught, and finally James summed it all up. His two main points were, first, that God was already saving Gentiles without reference to any ritual or law of any kind, and second, that this was the genuine activity of God because it agreed with the Word of God. So, as James put together the actions of God and the Word of God, the council came to the unanimous conclusion that this was indeed the mind of the Spirit. They realized that God was in their midst and that he could make his mind known to them. They understood that when they reached unanimity of opinion, they had found the mind of the Spirit. The first principle of guidance from God that is revealed here, especially in doctrinal matters, is that unanimous agreement in line with the Word marks the mind of the Spirit.

Notice also that they conveyed this decision to the people in Antioch not only by letter, but also by appointing some men to go down and explain the letter to them. I write that kind of letter too; they have to be explained when people receive them! This letter, however, was perfectly clear; God was simply underscoring a very important lesson. People learn best by having truth presented both through the avenue of the eye and of the ear. These men were sent to expound the letter that was written, so as to make it perfectly clear to all. Some people learn better through reading, some through hearing.

Here we read of the beginning of a process for teaching in the church which is still God's method today. This is exactly what he has done with us. He has written us a letter, the Bible; he has put his truth in writing. He has also appointed men to come and explain it: teachers, gifted men who are able to expound the Scriptures. These include not only men who have been to seminaries, but many others as well, who have gifts of exhorting and teaching and preaching. So these men came to Antioch with this dual conveyance of the truth, because they had discovered the mind of the Spirit through the principle of unanimous agreement.

The Basic Activity

The second principle is set forth in the following paragraph:

So when they were sent off, they went down to An-

> tioch; and having gathered the congregation together, they delivered the letter. And when they had read it, they rejoiced at the exhortation. And Judas and Silas, who were themselves prophets, exhorted the brethren with many words and strengthened them. And after they had spent some time, they were sent off in peace by the brethren to those who had sent them. But Paul and Barnabas remained in Antioch, teaching and preaching the word of the Lord, with many others also (Acts 15:30-35).

What a sigh of relief went up from these Gentile Christians when the letter arrived! They would not have to be subject to any Jewish ritual. They had understood this already from the teaching of Paul, but now it was very apparent that the whole church was in agreement. How delighted they were at this confirming exhortation!

But now notice how this paragraph focuses upon the activity of believers when there is no special guidance from the Holy Spirit to do something new or unusual. Judas and Silas came down with Paul and Barnabas, and they spent their time "exhorting the brethren with many words and strengthening them." This is what you do between the occasions of extraordinary activity in the Spirit-filled life. You give yourself to the most fundamental and basic activity of Christianity, the knowledge and understanding of the Word of God, the learning of the Word. This is always in order, always in season. So is the teaching and preaching of the Word, as you see in the last sentence: "But Paul and Barnabas remained in Antioch, teaching and preaching the Word of the Lord. . . ." But don't miss the last four words: "with many others also." In that congregation there were many, beside the four men mentioned here, who had gifts of teaching and preaching. They exercised them there in Antioch and in all the area around.

The Way the Word Spreads

In every congregation or community of believers there are many people who have the gift of teaching and the gift of preaching (proclaiming the truth, telling it abroad and appealing to the will—as opposed to teaching, which instructs the mind). If you have these gifts, you should be exercising them, just as they did in Antioch. This is the secret of the multiplication of the church. As they did this in Antioch, the word spread throughout the surrounding region.

Several years ago I had the privilege of being in a party which visited the ruins of Baalbek, located between the Lebanon ranges, between Beirut and Damascus. In the valley between those high mountain ranges a strong civilization had developed in these early centuries. At the foot of the valley, on the Orontes River, is Antioch, the very city we are reading about here. In the first century, Christian communities sprang up all through that valley. I walked around the ruins of Baalbek and noted how vast and extensive this complex is. It is one of the largest in the world, with a temple to Jupiter; a temple to Bacchus, the god of wine; one to Venus, goddess of sex; and a number of temples to other gods, covering a huge area. I asked the guide when these temples were at their height and was most interested in his reply. He said they were built by the Romans in the first century A.D. to counteract the spread of Christianity through this area.

The Romans went to great expense and effort to build these huge pagan temples. They went down to Egypt and quarried the stones for the columns, painfully moved them across the desert sands on rollers, floated them down the Nile river, shipped the huge pillars across the Mediterranean, and dragged them up the valley or over the mountain ranges. It was a tremendous, herculean task. They did it in desperation, to stop the spread of Christianity throughout that whole region. And who was spreading it? The people were, as they exercised their gifts and were obedient to this second principle of the Spirit's guidance: when you do not know what else to do, persist in learning and teaching the Word of God. That is fundamental to everything else.

Responsible Concern

Now look at a third principle:

And after some days Paul said to Barnabas, "Come, let us return and visit the brethren in every city where we proclaimed the word of the Lord, and see how they are" (Acts 15:36).

There is no vision here, no angelic call. There is no lightning, no special word of the Spirit in the inner heart. There is simply the responsible concern of Paul and Barnabas for the people whom they had led to Christ. They remembered all those Gentiles who had come to Christ in the cities of Antioch of Pisidia, Iconium, Lystra, and Derbe, and they said to one another, "We have a responsibility to help them grow in grace. They do not yet know the whole counsel of God; there are truths that they must understand, without which they will be lacking in their Christian experience. Let us go and see how they are, and impart these truths to them."

This is a perfectly proper leading of the Holy Spirit. God does not want to give orders to you about everything you do, as we saw illustrated in Acts 13. Once you discover the power by which to act—the life of Jesus within, ready to respond to the choice of your will—then the initiative lies with you. You can do what lies on your heart to do. If you sense an opportunity to show responsible concern for another person, move into it, and God will be with you in it.

There is a fourth principle in the next paragraph:

And Barnabas wanted to take with them John called Mark. But Paul thought best not to take with them one who had withdrawn from them in Pamphylia, and had not gone with them to the work. And there arose a sharp contention, so that they separated from each other; Barnabas took Mark with him and sailed away to Cyprus, but Paul chose Silas and departed, being commended by the brethren to the grace of the Lord. And he went through Syria and Cilicia, strengthening the churches (Acts 15:37-41).

This quarrel between Barnabas and Paul has fascinated many. These two men could not agree on whether to take young John Mark with them again. Barnabas was Mark's cousin and wanted to give the young man another chance. But Paul did not want to take the risk; the work was both important and dangerous, and he did not think it wise to take someone they could not count on. So we read the sad note that "there arose a sharp contention between them." Many have said, "Which of these men was right?" Disagreements have arisen over *this* question, so that many people have had "sharp contention" between them over whether Paul or Barnabas was right!

Agree to Disagree

But this is really not the point. I believe that *both* of these men were right. One was looking at the work and the other at the person. As Paul looked at the work he was perfectly right to say, "We don't want somebody who is apt to cop out on us." And he probably quoted the words of Jesus, "If any man puts his hand to the plow and turns back, he is not worthy of the kingdom of God." Christian service and ministry *are* demanding, and those who undertake them should be prepared to go through with the work and stick with it to the end, for God's cause is injured by those who quit in the middle.

On the other hand, Barnabas (though I'm sure he would have agreed as to the importance of the work) was looking at the young man. He knew that Mark was gifted. Sure, he had failed, but who doesn't? Who of us does not need a second chance, does not need to have a forgiving spirit exercised toward us, and the opportunity to try again? So Barnabas was willing to give Mark a second chance.

This situation indicates a very normal and proper procedure by which we may know the mind of the Spirit. There are times when there are differences of viewpoint which require a separation. The will of God was that Barnabas should take Mark and go to Cyprus, because Cyprus, his birthplace, had not been visited since the churches there had been founded. And it was equally the will of God for Paul to take Silas and go into Syria and Cilicia, because the churches there needed his particular ministry. But it was not the will of God that they should be sharp in their contention. It was the will of God to separate; it was not the will of God to quarrel. There are indeed times when the Spirit of God leads Christians to go separate ways. But they should do so with joy and with an agreeable understanding that the mind of the Spirit has been expressed in their divergent viewpoints.

Still another principle, the fifth, is in Chapter 16, as we ignore the chapter division and move right on:

> **And he came also to Derbe and to Lystra. A disciple was there, named Timothy, the son of a Jewish woman who was a believer; but his father was a Greek. He was well spoken of by the brethren at Lystra and Iconium. Paul wanted Timothy to accompany him; and he took him and circumcised him because of the Jews that were in those places, for they all knew that his father was a Greek. As they went on their way through the cities, they delivered to them for observance the decisions which had been reached by the apostles and elders who were at Jerusalem. So the churches were strengthened in the faith, and they increased in numbers daily (Acts 16:1-5).**

Paul is now back at Lystra, the city where he had been stoned, where he had encountered the most severe opposition of his first missionary journey. On that first occasion he had led a young man to Christ, who was now still only a boy, about sixteen years old. Paul thought he observed in him various gifts—gifts of ministry, perhaps of wisdom and knowledge in the Scriptures, of teaching, and of preaching. He wanted to take Timothy with him, using that marvelous means of discipling which has never been superseded. It was the process and method by which Jesus himself trained men, taking them along with him and teaching them as they ministered together. So Paul took Timothy as an intern on the rest of his journey.

The Underlying Principle

But there was a bit of a problem. Timothy was half Jewish, half Greek. His father was a Greek but his mother was a Jew, and according to the Jews this made him a Jew. The Jewish people had a very practical way of thinking about this: anyone knows who a man's mother is, but you can't be as sure of his father. So they reckoned the line of descent through the mother, and Timothy was therefore considered a Jew.

The amazing thing is that Paul circumcised Timothy, while earlier he had refused to do the same to Titus. Here is another marvelous indication of how to know the mind and will of God. In any situation involving customs and rituals—cultural matters—the governing rule is to find the great underlying principle at stake, and to act according to that principle. In the case of Titus, it would have been devastating to have circumcised him. It would have meant yielding to the whole concept of legalism, and of initiating circumcision of Gentiles as a Christian teaching. Titus was entirely Greek, but Timothy's situation was different. Timothy was looked upon as a Jew, and in order not to offend the Jews among whom he must labor, in order to open the door of acceptance by them, Paul submits to this Old Testament ritual and circumcises Timothy. Here the governing principle, as expressed by Paul, is: "I have become all things to all men, that I might by all means save [win] some" (1 Cor. 9:22). This approach may result in two seemingly contradictory actions, but all is reconciled as you see the great principle underneath.

We have two more principles of guidance in the next paragraph:

> And they went through the region of Phrygia and Galatia, having been forbidden by the Holy Spirit to speak the word in Asia. And when they had come opposite Mysia, they attempted to go into Bithynia, but the Spirit of Jesus did not allow them; so, passing by Mysia, they went down to Troas (Acts 16:6-8).

What a remarkably helpful illustration this is! It links with what we said earlier—that the initiative lies with the Christian. Paul did not wait for directions from God as to where he was to go; he went to the most logical place. He went to where it appeared there was an open door, taking the next step on the path before him. But the Holy Spirit did not want him to go there, and so *he shut the door*.

A Voice Behind You

I fully believe these words indicate that Paul was experiencing what we call the "inner witness of the Spirit." The Spirit of God is willing to confirm to us, or deny to us, whether or not we have made a correct decision—but only after we make the decision. That is important to note. Isaiah said, "Your ears shall hear a word *behind* you, saying, 'This is the way, walk in it'" (Isa. 30:21). Behind you, after you have made the decision, after you have started out, *then* there will be a voice which says, "Yes, this is right." That "voice" is usually a sense of peace, a great inner sense of the confirming peace of the Holy Spirit which, after you have committed yourself, tells you it is right.

But suppose the decision is not correct. Well then, it is not wrong to try. Paul is not rebuked here because he tried to go into Asia or Bithynia. That was perfectly all right. The Spirit simply said, "No, Paul, the time is not yet." Later Paul did go into Asia, where Ephesus is located. But the Spirit's timing is not yet.

So, not waiting for any particular directions but moving out, Paul is guided of the Spirit by the closing of doors, or by the inner sense of denial from the Spirit, and thus he is led at last to the city of Troas. This is near the ancient city of Troy, whose people fought the Trojan wars against the Greeks. Now look what happens to Paul in this ancient city:

> **And a vision appeared to Paul in the night: a man of Macedonia was standing beseeching him and saying, "Come over to Macedonia and help us." And when he had seen the vision, immediately we sought to go on into Macedonia, concluding that God had called us to preach the gospel to them (Acts 16:9, 10).**

God is sovereign, and he can choose the way he wants to direct you. Sometimes he will come through in such an unmistakable way that you cannot help but know that God has spoken. Something like that occurred when I first became pastor of Peninsula Bible Church. My name was suggested by three different sources, none of whom knew that the others were writing. Each wrote independently and yet their letters all arrived in the same week. The men who had to decide were not considering any other man at the time, and when they went to the mailbox they found these three letters suggesting that they get in touch with a young man named Ray Stedman. That was a clear-cut moving of the Spirit of God, and they took it as such.

So here is a vision from God. Notice that it is not a dream. The difference between a dream and a vision is that a dream always has *us* in it—which may make it a nightmare! Psychologists tell us that dreams always involve ourselves. If you dreamed last night of a long-eared mule, or a witch on a broomstick, or whatever, that was you. You were in the center of the dream. But this is a vision: it is not of Paul, but another man, a Macedonian, calling out to him, "Come over and help us." Paul knew it to be a vision. "And [I love this] *immediately* we sought to go on into Macedonia, concluding that God had called us to preach the gospel to them." They make an immediate response. Do you see the quiet acting of faith here? Paul expects God to lead him. He does not doubt it. He simply acts on the matters before him and expects God to correct him if he is wrong. He is already moving out, but he determines his exact destination on the basis of the vision that he had seen.

And notice something else interesting here. This is where Luke joins the party. In verse 8 Luke says ". . . *they* went down to Troas." But when you come to verse 10, it is "And when he had seen the vision, immediately *we* sought to go on into Macedonia, concluding that God had called *us* to preach. . . ." By that change in pronouns from *they* to *we*, Luke indicates that he has now joined the expedition. We don't know where he came from, or how he got there, or what contact he had with Paul. Perhaps in one of these Greek cities along the way Luke had met the apostle. Now he joins him and is united with Paul as they reach out toward Europe. In our next study, we will be looking at the way the gospel came into Europe and thus changed all of Western civilization, vastly affecting our lives today.

These are some of the ways God guides. Let me review them briefly. In the understanding of doctrine he guides by *unanimous agreement*. In those quiet periods of life, when there is no particular sense of direction from any source, he expects us to manifest *persistent obedience* in learning, teaching, and exhorting in the Word. In relations with other persons he expects us to show a *responsible concern*, which will often initiate action. In irreconcilable practical differences of opinion he expects *cordial separation*, so that there is unity of spirit even though there is no longer union of endeavor. In customs, rituals, and cultural matters he expects us to examine the *important principle at stake* and to act according to that. Finally, in matters of geographical direction, we saw two ways that he guides: either by denying to us or confirming to us by *a sense of peace*, the most obvious and legitimate action to take; or by a direct and obvious interposition of his mind and will, made known through *a vision or a call* that is unmistakably from God.

Who knows how God will guide you? You can understand some of the possibilities from our study here. But the important thing is that above all, whatever action you take, you do it on the basis of dependence upon his power in you, his life in you. "Whatsoever you do in word or deed, do all to the glory of the Lord." The only thing that glorifies God is God at work. Only God can do God's work. Only God can glorify himself.

> **Please teach us, heavenly Father, how to apply this practical help which the Scriptures so freely give us in our daily life. May it be true of us that we are available instruments, ready to be used according to your mind and purpose, right where we are—not waiting for anything dramatic but ready to move out, knowing that you will lead us and work through us, as you have promised to do. We thank you in Jesus' name, Amen.**

CHAPTER SIX

D-DAY AT PHILIPPI

Acts 16:11-40

Now we come to an obscure and apparently minor event which, in the reckoning of hindsight, has turned out to be one of the most significant and momentous occasions in human history. It is the story of the entrance of the gospel into Europe. When the Apostle Paul and his small company crossed the Dardanelles, moving from Asia to Europe, they changed the whole course of Western civilization. Perhaps no single event since the cross of Christ has so affected the world as Paul's seemingly insignificant decision to cross a narrow neck of water. If the Emperor Claudius, who occupied the throne in Rome at that time, had been asked to name the most significant event of his reign, I'm sure he would never have dreamed of suggesting (had he even known about it) that it was the occasion when an obscure little bald-headed Jew decided to leave Asia for Europe. That is how little we understand the history we are living through! We don't know what the really great events are.

The Apostle Paul, with his faithful friend Silas and his young follower Timothy, had been joined by Dr. Luke in the city of Troas. There Paul had a vision of a man from Macedonia asking him to come over and help, and the apostle never waited a moment. Whenever he found a

door open he tried to move through it. As Luke tells us
what happened, we will see unfolding once again the
familiar pattern followed by these early Christians in
planting the gospel in new places.

> Setting sail therefore from Troas, we made a direct
> voyage to Samothrace, and the following day to
> Neapolis, and from there to Philippi, which is the
> leading city of the district of Macedonia, and a
> Roman colony. We remained in this city some days;
> and on the sabbath day we went outside the gate to
> the riverside, where we supposed there was a place
> of prayer; and we sat down and spoke to the women
> who had come together (Acts 16:11-13).

Not a very impressive beginning, is it? Here are Paul
and Silas and their company in this pagan city of Philippi. Luke is careful to tell us that it was a Roman colony,
because the Philippians prided themselves in this fact.
About a century earlier a great battle had been fought
outside the walls of the city, in which Brutus and Cassius,
the murderers of Julius Caesar, had been defeated by the
combined forces of Antony and Octavian, who later
became the Emperor Augustus. Because of the help they
gave to Octavian's armies, Octavian granted Roman
citizenship to these Philippians when he became
emperor. Therefore the city became a little bit of Rome
transplanted to far-off Macedonia. The people had all
the rights of every Roman citizen and were governed in
the same way as Rome. They were proud of their status
as a Roman colony located so far from the capital.

When Paul and Silas and the others came into the
city they were faced with the problem of how to start a
Christian work. But this was no real problem to Paul.
Everywhere he went he always began with the same

activity—simply proclaiming the revolutionary message about Jesus, the word about Christ.

Most Influential People

They *did* have to choose where to begin, however. Philippi was a pagan city, evidently with too few male Jews to have a synagogue. The law was very specific: you had to have ten adult male Jews in order to have a synagogue. If there were not that many, then the law provided that the Jewish people were to meet by a river and have a prayer meeting.

That is why Paul, Silas, Timothy, and Luke walked along the riverside on their first sabbath morning in Philippi—to see if they could find a Jewish prayer meeting. To their delight they did. But, perhaps to their dismay, they found that the only people present were women. It was through a women's club that the gospel entered Europe! Perhaps this doesn't seem to be a very promising beginning. Most of us would feel that the way to start evangelizing a city is to gather the most influential people together. But, as a matter of fact, that is exactly what they did! The most influential people in any community are the women, and I'm not joking when I say that. They have a power to work behind the scenes that is absolutely unparalleled. So Paul and Silas, led of God, found the opportunity to address these women by the riverside, where they began to preach the gospel—as always, to the most available people.

The second principle they followed was immediately evident:

One who heard us was a woman named Lydia, from the city of Thyatira, a seller of purple goods, who

was a worshiper of God. The Lord opened her heart to give heed to what was said by Paul. And when she was baptized, with her household, she besought us, saying, "If you have judged me to be faithful to the Lord, come to my house and stay." And she prevailed upon us (Acts 16:14, 15).

The next step after proclaiming the Word of God is always up to God. These disciples expected *God* to do something! That, by the way, is the missing note among Christians in many places today. Many churches have given up expecting God to do anything, for *they* expect to do everything. It is literally true, as someone has observed, that many churches today are operating in such a way that, if the Holy Spirit were suddenly removed from their program, nobody would notice the difference. They do not expect God to do anything, but these people did. They preached the Word and then expected God to act.

Prepared by God

They could not tell what God would do—he is always unpredictable. Philippi was a tough nut to crack, so God employed four different methods to open that town. Although he is by no means limited to these four, they are ones he frequently uses.

First, he prepared men and women in that city, people whose hearts were ready to respond to the gospel. Such a woman was Lydia, who was already a worshiper of God. She was a business woman who sold purple goods, dealing in the purple dye for cloth which was so valuable in those days. She made a good living and had her own home, which was large enough to accommodate Paul and his party. Her heart was ready, having been prepared by God, and she was led of God to be there and to hear.

When I have had the occasional privilege of speaking to groups of non-Christians, who have given me a cold and rather hostile eye at times, and whose reactions I couldn't anticipate, it has been a great encouragement to my heart to realize that there are unquestionably people in the group whom God has prepared. I never doubt it, for I have always found that there are at least one or two. I talk to them and try to ignore the hostile reaction of the others.

This is what happened here. Lydia was there and she did not get upset by the message. She did not view it as a challenge to her Jewish faith, but immediately recognized that it was the fulfillment of all her Jewish hopes. So she opened her heart and received the Lord. Then God employed another of his methods to crack open a city:

> As we were going to the place of prayer, we were met by a slave girl who had a spirit of divination and brought her owner much gain by soothsaying. She followed Paul and us, crying, "These men are servants of the Most High God, who proclaim to you the way of salvation." And this she did for many days. But Paul was annoyed, and turned and said to the spirit, "I charge you in the name of Jesus Christ to come out of her." And it came out that very hour (Acts 16:16-18).

One of the ways God arrests people's attention is by a spectacular deliverance like this. Sometimes it is in the realm of the physical, as when Paul, preaching at Lystra, saw a man lame from birth and said to him, "Rise, stand upon your feet; Jesus Christ makes you well." And sometimes, as in this case, it is in the realm of the spirit.

This teenage girl, a slave, whom today we would call a medium or even a witch, was possessed by an evil spirit who used her as a channel to convey clairvoyant messages, interpreting various events of the day and predicting the future for people. She was exploited for revenue by a group of unscrupulous owners. This girl followed Paul and the others around and declared wherever they went: "These men are servants of the Most High God, who proclaim to you the way of salvation."

Platform for Subversion

Actually this was a very dangerous, satanic attack upon the gospel. The devil knows the power of the Word of God, and he knew what these men could do in Philippi if they got a chance. So he was already prepared to adopt his most powerful tactic: to derail their proclamation right at the beginning by appearing to be in line with it, by attempting to form an alliance and thus gaining a position from which eventually to subvert the whole program.

The devil has only two basic approaches: either apparent alliance or outright attack—one or the other. Of the two, alliance is by far the more dangerous because it appears to be so helpful. What this girl said was perfectly, absolutely true. These men were indeed servants of the Most High God, and had indeed come to declare the way of salvation.

So, you might ask, why didn't they welcome this? For

the same reason that Jesus never allowed a person possessed of an evil spirit to give testimony to him. In the Gospels we are told that wherever Jesus went, the evil spirits would cry out, "Thou art the Son of the Most High God!" And Jesus would always rebuke them, saying, "Hold your peace."

Why? For two reasons: first, if men were drawn to him on that basis, they would be coming with a wrong motive. Anyone who deals with mediums, witches, astrology, or any aspect of the occult is always motivated by self-interest. They want to use these forces to benefit themselves in some way. Second, it would not be very long before the truth, which was originally proclaimed as bait to lead people on, would be mixed with error, and very serious error at that. Then people would be sucked in so that they could no longer tell the difference between truth and error. That is the story of every cult that bears the name of Christianity in the world today. They all began with a proclamation of truth, but soon error began to be intermingled, and eventually people were led right off the track.

Someone once sent me a book titled *Edgar Cayce's Story of Jesus*. Perhaps you know who Edgar Cayce was; he lived earlier in this century and was called "the sleeping prophet." He would go into a trance and pour out volumes of information supposedly from the spirit world. He has been hailed as a leading prophet of our generation. Because *some* of his predictions came true, he is regarded, even by some Christians (unfortunately) as an authoritative spokesman. His followers have now published this book, in which he takes the facts of the New Testament and interweaves with them a lot of spiritualistic revelations and clairvoyant readings. It is a mishmash of spiritism and Christianity, all designed to first attract people with the truth and then lead them into error.

That is why Paul was annoyed. The word "annoyed" might seem to suggest that Paul was merely irritated by this woman who kept following him around. But the word actually means "deeply troubled." Paul was deeply troubled because he knew what would happen if he allowed or recognized her testimony. So finally, in the power of the Spirit of God, he turned and said, "I charge you in the name of Jesus Christ to come out of her." The spirit came out that very hour, and the girl was set free.

Violence Allowed

It must have been a tremendous blessing to her heart to be delivered from this evil thing. But, as always, the devil was quick to twist everything to his own ends. That which was a blessing to this girl he immediately employed to awaken serious opposition, just as he did after the healing of the lame man in Lystra. But remember that one of God's ways of opening a community is to allow the devil to arouse violent opposition. Look what happens now:

> But when her owners saw that their hope of gain was gone, they seized Paul and Silas and dragged them into the market place before the rulers; and when they had brought them to the magistrates they said, "These men are Jews and they are disturbing our city. They advocate customs which it is not lawful for us Romans to accept or practice." The crowd joined in attacking them; and the magistrates tore the garments off them and gave orders to beat them with rods. And when they had inflicted many blows

upon them, they threw them into prison, charging the jailer to keep them safely. Having received this charge, he put them into the inner prison and fastened their feet in the stocks (Acts 16:19-24).

God permitted this opposition in order to open a door for a church to be implanted in this city. This may appear to be a self-contradictory statement, but think this through with me. When Paul and his men preached the message of truth in Philippi, opposition mounted rapidly, soon erupting in outright violence. Why? This was a sure sign that one of the enemy's strongholds was being attacked. Philippi was a place where evil was long-standing and deeply imbedded. The enemy knew that when this stronghold fell, the whole surrounding area would be open to the gospel. "The weapons of our warfare are not worldly but have divine power to destroy strongholds" (2 Cor. 10:4). That is why there was so much opposition. But by allowing it to happen, God was laying the groundwork for further steps in his plan to deliver the city of Philippi.

The particular stronghold of evil at Philippi found its expression in the pride of the citizens in their status as a Roman colony. Notice how clever the owners of this girl were. They immediately hauled Paul and Silas before the magistrates on the charge that they were challenging the rights of Romans. "They advocate customs which it is not lawful for us Romans to accept or practice." Paul and Silas had touched their point of pride, and their reaction was no longer logical but emotional. A lynch mob formed immediately over this emotional issue.

The crowd responded wildly, and, as calculated, the magistrates were swept off their feet, with the end result that Paul and Silas were beaten. According to the official Roman punishment, their backs were bared and they were beaten with rods as thick as a man's thumb until their backs were bloody and raw. Then the magistrates charged the jailer to put them into the innermost cell of the dungeon. In the darkness and dampness he locked their feet in stocks so they couldn't even turn over. This violent reaction shows how deeply the power of evil was entrenched in this town.

Singing at Midnight

But we have not yet come to the end of the story. The fourth method God uses here is dramatic intervention.

> **But about midnight Paul and Silas were praying and singing hymns to God, and the prisoners were listening to them, and suddenly there was a great earthquake, so that the foundations of the prison were shaken; and immediately all the doors were opened and every one's fetters were unfastened (Acts 16:25, 26).**

There is nothing unusual about an earthquake in this region; to this day earthquakes are common in northern Macedonia. It was the *timing* of it that was supernatural. God released the earthquake, precipitating it precisely at the right moment and thus setting Paul, Silas, and the other prisoners free. The most dramatic aspect of this story, though, is not the earthquake, nor the fact that the prison was damaged and fetters unfastened. It is the singing of Paul and Silas at midnight. Somebody has said that the gospel entered Europe through a sacred concert which was so successful that it brought the house down!

Frankly, I am filled with admiration for these men. Imagine—they were praising God! (That is the meaning of the word "praying" here.) They were not asking for anything; they were praising God and singing hymns. They were not faking either. Their backs were raw and bloody, and they had suffered a great injustice. They were facing agonizing uncertainty, with no way of knowing that this delivering earthquake was coming (since they had not requested it), but they exhibited no self-pity or resentment.

All this is accentuated by the solemn words "at midnight." Everything—pain and heartache and disappointment—is always the worst at midnight. But it was at midnight that they began praising God and singing hymns. I don't know what they sang. I know what *I* would be singing: "Rescue the Perishing, Care for the Dying"! But they were probably singing "How Great Thou Art!" Evidently they sang because they could see things that we in our poor, blinded condition seldom see. These were men of faith, and I think I know some of what they saw. When you see it, you will no longer ask, "Why did they sing?" but, "What else could they do but sing?"

They saw, first, that the enemy had panicked. Paul and Silas and all these other early Christians were always conscious of what Paul describes in Ephesians 6: that we are battling not against flesh and blood but against principalities and powers and wicked spirits in high places. This is a spiritual battle which is tough and demanding, and where every inch of the way will be contested. But they were delighted when they saw that the enemy had resorted to violence, because that always means that he has already emptied his bag of tricks. He is down to the bottom of the barrel, and there is nothing left. They knew they had won.

The second thing they saw was that God, in his resurrection power, was at work in the situation. Resurrection power cannot be stopped. As Paul would later write to these Philippians, "What has happened to me has really served to advance the gospel." All attempts to oppose the gospel, or to throw an obstacle in its path, are turned around and used as opportunities for advancement. Paul and Silas knew this, and so they were assured that the work was established, that it would continue, and that they had won. Resurrection power was at work.

The Privilege of Suffering

The third thing they understood in all this was that suffering—physical, mental, and emotional suffering—is absolutely necessary to Christian maturity. They themselves had been benefited by this experience. Again, Paul would write to these same Philippians and say,

For it has been granted to you that for the sake of Christ you should not only believe in him but also suffer for his sake (Phil. 1:29).

Suffering is part of the program. They knew this was so because it was part of the program for the Son of God. The writer of the Letter to the Hebrews says,

Although he was a Son, he learned obedience through what he suffered; and being made perfect he

became the source of eternal salvation to all who obey him (Heb. 5:8, 9).

Suffering is an absolutely inescapable part of the curriculum. You will never grow up, you will never be what God wants you to be, without some form of suffering. When you learn that, you will start rejoicing when you encounter suffering, as these men rejoiced. They saw that the foe had been defeated, that the work was established, and that they personally had benefited. So they began to rejoice and sing and thank God for what they saw. The heart of God was so blessed by this that he said, "I just can't hold still; I'm going to shake the place up a bit!"

Now we see the next step in the pattern. According to their established routine they had come to town and proclaimed the Word; they had expected God to do something, and then, when the results began to show, they started the operation of body life—the life of the family of God. This is what happened:

When the jailer woke and saw that the prison doors were open, he drew his sword and was about to kill himself, supposing that the prisoners had escaped. But Paul cried with a loud voice, "Do not harm yourself, for we are all here." And he called for lights and rushed in, and trembling with fear he fell down before Paul and Silas, and brought them out and said, "Men, what must I do to be saved?" And they said, "Believe in the Lord Jesus, and you will be saved, you and your household." And they spoke the word of the Lord to him and to all that were in his house. And he took them the same hour of the night, and washed their wounds, and he was baptized at once, with all his family. Then he brought them up

**into his house, and set food before them; and he
rejoiced with all his household that he had believed
in God (Acts 16:27-34).**

The result is that a church is formed right there. They
had reached some women before, but a church must include both men and women, as well as all classes of
society. Here were the men—the jailer and his family
and household, servants and all.

They came because of the crisis in this jailer's life.
There are some who read these words of the jailer, "Men,
what must I do to be saved?" as though he were saying,
"Men, how do I get out of this mess? How do I square
myself with the authorities?" But I am confident that this
is not what he is asking, because the answer of Paul and
Silas is, "If you believe in the Lord Jesus, you will be
saved, you and your household." The household was not
in trouble with the magistrates; the jailer was. So he must
be talking about eternal things. If you refer to what had
just happened to him, you can see why. He thought his
prisoners were free, and he knew that his own life would
be taken if they got away. So, rather than allow the
authorities to take his life he was going to do it himself.
He had drawn his sword and was ready to plunge it into
his breast. He was about to die when Paul stopped him
with the dramatic words, "Do not harm yourself, for we
are all here."

When men are about to die they start thinking about
what lies beyond. That is what is behind the jailer's
question. Paul and Silas responded with the only possible
answer: "Believe in the Lord Jesus, and you will be
saved, you and your household." The word "believe"
governs the entire sentence. If his household believes,
they too will be saved. They are not saved because this

man believed; they will be saved when *they* believe. Paul and Silas spoke the word of the Lord to him *and* to all that were in his house. They all believed, so they were all saved, and that was the beginning of God's family in Philippi.

The immediate reaction of the jailer was to wash their wounds. What a beautiful picture! This man who just a few hours before had thrown them in the cell and had brutally locked them in stocks was now washing their wounds, sponging away all the blood and dirt and filth and tenderly taking care of the men to whom he had been joined in the family of God. That is the beginning of body life—the immediate sharing of one another's problems, the bearing of one another's burdens. They also rejoiced together, which is another aspect of body life. In a great time of celebration they welcomed each other into the family of God.

For the Sake of the Body

The last section continues the theme of the beginning of body life, and it must be read in that context in order to be understood.

> But when it was day, the magistrates sent the police, saying, "Let those men go." And the jailer reported the words to Paul, saying, "The magistrates have sent to let you go; now therefore come out and go in peace." But Paul said to them, "They have beaten us publicly, uncondemned, men who are Roman citizens, and have thrown us into prison; and now do they cast us out secretly? No! let them come themselves and take us out." The police reported these words to the magistrates, and they were afraid

when they heard that they were Roman citizens; so they came and apologized to them. And they took them out and asked them to leave the city. So they went out of the prison, and visited Lydia; and when they had seen the brethren, they exhorted them and departed (Acts 16:35-40).

There is humor in Paul's response here. The police told Paul he could go, but he said, "No! We're not going. They beat us, though uncondemned, breaking the law themselves. Now let them come down and ask us to leave." And so these magistrates, who had just cast them into prison, came down, hats in hand, and apologized for their treatment of these two, and begged them to leave town. Paul said, "Very well, we'll leave, but we'll take our time about it. We want to have lunch with Lydia first, and then we'll visit some of the brethren."

Who are the brethren? This is the first mention of any male converts here in Philippi other than the jailer. One time, after I had preached a message on this passage, a delightful college student came up to me and asked, "Who were these brethren?" I told him I didn't know, and he said, "Do you know who I think they were? I think they were the prisoners who had been listening to Paul and Silas sing at midnight." I think he was right. We are not told what happened to them, but the prisoners *were* listening intently, and they too were freed by this event.

You might ask, "Why did Paul raise the issue of his Roman citizenship at this point?" Some think he was being a bit prickly and difficult, somewhat vengeful for his own sake. But we must read this in the context of what he is doing with the body of Christ here at Philippi. He could have invoked his status in his own defense much earlier. Had he mentioned that he was a Roman citizen when they were about to beat him, he probably could have spared himself the beating. He did not say a word then, but now he does, for the sake of the Christians in the city of Philippi. You can see what a difference it made for these magistrates to come down to the prison and apologize to Paul and Silas, and to publicly acknowledge their illegal treatment. This put the church on an entirely different standing within the community. So it is clear that Paul did this for the sake of the body.

His final act is to gather the brethren together and to exhort them, teach them, and admonish them to go on in the Lord. When you read the Letter to the Philippians, written from Paul's Roman prison—again in prison, still rejoicing—you can see that this letter is full of triumph. He is still exhorting the believers to rejoice, still teaching them and ministering to the body. That is a principle the early Christians always followed. The minute believers came together they began sharing one another's burdens, praying for one another, rejoicing together, and living together the life of Jesus Christ. It is crucially important for the church to recover this again in our own day.

Father, we pray that we will demonstrate the life of Christ not only in some outward, external fashion, but most of all in the way we accept one another, pray for one another, seek to help one another, bear one another's burdens, and meet one another's needs. Lord, help us to brighten the hearts and lives of lonely people around us by our warmth and willingness to share something of the joy we have together. We ask it in Jesus' name, Amen.

CHAPTER SEVEN

RABBLE AND NOBLES
Acts 17:1-15

Once God had established a bridgehead in the midst of
the entrenched evil of Philippi, he then moved Paul and
Silas westward, leaving Luke and Timothy behind in
Philippi for the time being.

> Now when they had passed through Amphipolis and
> Appollonia, they came to Thessalonica, where there
> was a synagogue of the Jews. And Paul went in, as
> was his custom, and for three weeks he argued with
> them from the scriptures, explaining and proving
> that it was necessary for the Christ to suffer and to
> rise from the dead, and saying, "This Jesus, whom I
> proclaim to you, is the Christ." And some of them
> were persuaded, and joined Paul and Silas; as did a
> great many of the devout Greeks and not a few of the
> leading women (Acts 17:1-4).

Paul and Silas were following the famous Roman road
called the Egnatian Way, which crossed Macedonia and
connected the Adriatic Sea with the Black Sea. The cities
mentioned here all lie on that road. Here we see
something of the apostle's strategy as he was led of the
Spirit to move into various cities, passing through some
and stopping in others. He always chose the most

strategic center from which the gospel might reach out into the surrounding area.

In this particular region it was Thessalonica. I once visited that city, and as I stood on the old Roman wall which formed the northern city limits I could see the old Via Egnatia winding down out of the hills into the city proper. In my mind's eye I could picture Paul and Silas and the little band of Christian brethren coming down that road into the city.

You might get the impression from this account that this journey was a rather pleasant afternoon's stroll. But Amphipolis is 33 miles from Philippi, a long day's journey on foot. Apollonia is some 30 miles from Amphipolis, another day's journey. Thessalonica is 37 miles beyond Apollonia, and that is also a long day's journey. It must have taken Paul at least three days to trudge from Philippi to Thessalonica, even though Luke dismisses this hundred-mile trek with just a sentence.

When they entered Thessalonica they first found a synagogue of the Jews, and for three sabbath mornings Paul reasoned with them out of the Scriptures. He was undoubtedly in the city much longer than three weeks, but he was limited to three weeks' ministry within the synagogue itself. He was soon excluded from teaching further there, as we will see. If you wonder what he was doing the rest of the week, he tells us in Second Thessalonians:

> For you yourselves know how you ought to imitate us; we were not idle when we were with you, we did not eat any one's bread without paying, but with toil and labor we worked night and day, that we might not burden any of you (2 Thess. 3:7, 8).

Paul made tents all through the week, but on Saturday

he went into the synagogue and taught. Using the Scriptures, he dealt with that great stumbling block to the Jews—the death and resurrection of Christ. These people, like Jews all over the world at that time, were having a great struggle over Jesus of Nazareth. They could only accept him as the Messiah if they were not confronted with the facts of his death. A suffering, crucified Messiah was a great offense to them.

Selective Reading

These Jews read their Scriptures much as we sometimes read ours. They picked out all the passages they liked and kept reading these over and over. Eventually they thought that this was all the Scriptures said about the Messiah. They liked the passages which dealt with the majesty of the Messiah, when he would come in his royal power and establish his kingdom over all the world. They expected him to come and subdue all enemies, cause war and strife to cease, and reign in triumphant splendor and glory.

But they ignored those passages which dealt with a suffering and crucified Messiah, and with the necessity for a resurrection. Some of the Jewish rabbis had actually come up with the idea that there were two Messiahs. One they called Messhiach ben David (that is, Messiah the son of David). This was the glorious, triumphant king. Another they called Messhiach ben Joseph, from one Old Testament passage which some rabbis interpreted as teaching that the Messiah would be the son of Joseph, and that *he* would be the suffering One. Very likely this teaching is what John the Baptist had in mind when he was in prison. Discouraged, he sent word to Jesus, "Are you he who is to come, or should we look for another?"

Paul showed them there is only one. "This Jesus, whom I proclaim to you, is the Christ, the Messiah." I imagine he started with Isaiah 53:

> But he was wounded for our transgressions,
>   he was bruised for our iniquities;
> upon him was the chastisement that made us whole,
>   and with his stripes we are healed.
> All we like sheep have gone astray;
>   we have turned every one to his own way;
> and the Lord has laid upon him
>   the iniquity of us all (Isa. 53:5, 6).

What an impact he would have made with that passage! And perhaps he used Psalm 22, which opens with the words of Jesus from the cross: "My God, my God, why hast thou forsaken me?" This psalm goes on to describe the sufferings of his death, the agony that he went through. Then Paul must have brought in the resurrection passages, like Psalm 16: "For thou wilt not . . . permit thine Holy One to see corruption."

With passages such as these Paul reasoned with these Jews, proving that Jesus was the Christ. The account says, "And some of them were persuaded." Here we find three groups of people who responded to his message. The toughest nuts to crack were these religious Jews. In any community, religious people are always the most resistant. They are the ones most set in their ways, most prejudiced; they are the hardest to reach, because they think they know it all already. He reached only a few of these.

But there was also a great band of unprejudiced

Gentiles—Greeks who had tired of the emptiness of their pagan philosophies and had come to the synagogue hoping to hear the truth about the living God. They had been attracted by the Jewish Scriptures. They knew there was something here, but they had not yet become Jews and were not yet circumcised. As these Gentiles heard the word of the gospel they were tremendously impressed, and many believed.

Appeal to Women

Among them, Luke is careful to point out, was a group of the leading women of the city. You find this emphasis in several places in this book. This gospel had a particular appeal to women, especially to women of the upper classes, who were prominent citizens of these Greek cities. The reason was that these educated women, instructed in the philosophies of Greece, had found that the Greek philosophies were dead and empty, offering nothing for the heart or for the spirit within. They instructed the mind but did nothing for the soul. And further, they were philosophies full of voluptuous and degrading practices which left these women devastated and filled with self-loathing if they gave in to them. So they had turned from their philosophies to Judaism, only to find themselves burdened with difficult and cumbersome regulations which again left them empty.

Then the gospel came with the glad good news that in Jesus Christ there is neither male or female, bond nor free, black nor white, nor any other distinction, that all the distinctions men make were broken down, all the middle walls of partition removed. These women responded joyously! They found a liberating, fulfilling, and satisfying glory about the gospel, and they responded to the grace of God in Jesus Christ, inviting the Lord Jesus to enter their hearts. So there was a tremendous impact upon the city because of this conversion of a great band of Gentiles, including these leading women.

Rabble-Rousers

The devil, as you might expect by now, struck back immediately. The next section shows us what occurred when Paul and Silas had reached these people in the city with their preaching:

> But the Jews were jealous, and taking some wicked fellows of the rabble, they gathered a crowd, set the city in an uproar, and attacked the house of Jason, seeking to bring them out to the people. And when they could not find them, they dragged Jason and some of the brethren before the city authorities, crying, "These men who have turned the world upside down have come here also, and Jason has received them; and they are all acting against the decrees of Caesar, saying that there is another king, Jesus." And the people and the city authorities were disturbed when they heard this. And when they had taken security from Jason and the rest, they let them go (Acts 17:5-9).

We are told here that the Jews were jealous. They were unable to win against the power of the Scriptures and the logic of the apostles, and so they revealed the lawlessness in their own hearts by turning, literally, to "the loafers of the marketplace," young men who were what today we would call hoods or toughs—radicals who knew how to manipulate a crowd.

In this the Jews followed a classic pattern. They started a disturbance which attracted a crowd. When the crowd gathered around them, they inflamed them with emotional words and propaganda until the crowd was brought to a fever pitch. Then they gave them a victim to attack. They turned against Paul and Silas for no reason whatsoever. These Jews were skilled manipulators who could incite the people to an unprovoked and groundless attack upon the apostles. Here, as at Philippi, was another lynch mob.

But now notice how God works: he is fully in control, and just before the mob arrives he sends Paul and Silas out for a cup of coffee or something; they simply are not there when the crowd arrives. So the mob had to be satisfied with dragging Jason, the host, and some of the brethren, and bringing them before the city authorities.

The charges against Paul and Silas are very interesting. There is a germ of truth in them, but as a whole they are obviously false. They were charged, first, with being notorious troublemakers. "These men who have turned the world upside down have come here also." I don't know whether these authorities had heard aaout the trouble in Philippi or not. Perhaps they simply recognized Paul and Silas as Jews and, since the Jews were in trouble in Rome at that very time, they may have identified them with that trouble.

Whatever the reason, what they said was true: these were indeed men who had turned the world upside down. But what they didn't realize was that the world was *already* upside down! When you turn something up side down which is *already* upside down, you turn it right side up! The world was turned upside down at the fall of Adam, and it has been operating in reverse ever since. That is why it never works right. In the final analysis everything seems to fall apart. In spite of the best efforts of men, we are still struggling with the same problems men wrestled with in the days of Noah, before the flood. No progress whatsoever has been made, because the world is upside down.

But now the gospel comes in and turns it right side up. As men and women respond to the gospel, God's original intent for man begins to be worked out in their lives. Peace and tranquility and prosperity and progress and harmony and love and grace—all these wonderful things begin to flow out of a community which is operating in the fullness of life provided in Jesus Christ. So they were indeed men who turned the world upside down.

The second charge was that they were challenging Caesar's authority, that they were preaching another king—Jesus. Paul had in fact been declaring the kingship of Jesus, the fact that all men relate to him in some way. His spiritual kingdom encompasses the whole of humanity, and men live within that kingdom whether they like it or not. He is indeed Lord of all things, and men have a relationship to him. But of course these men interpreted that as a challenge to the authority of Caesar. They thought the apostles were political insurrectionists.

Paid to Leave Town

They finally settled the matter by taking security from Jason, which sounds as though Paul and Silas were released on bail. But if that is the case, they became bail jumpers, because immediately they went away by night to Berea. It is impossible to believe that Paul and Silas would try to cheat justice in this way. This must mean, then, that Jason had to give a certain amount of money as a guarantee that Paul and Silas would *leave* Thessalonica and never return. That is probably what Paul refers to in his First Letter to the Thessalonians:

> But since we were bereft of you, brethren, for a short time, in person not in heart, we endeavored the more eagerly and with great desire to see you face to face; because we wanted to come to you—I, Paul, again and again—but Satan hindered us (1 Thess. 2:17, 18).

What hindered him was very likely this guarantee against his return. The next stop is the city of Berea:

> The brethren immediately sent Paul and Silas away by night to Beroea; and when they arrived they went into the Jewish synagogue. Now these Jews were more noble than those in Thessalonica, for they received the word with all eagerness, examining the scriptures daily to see if these things were so. Many of them therefore believed, with not a few Greek women of high standing as well as men (Acts 17:10-12).

Berea is a very pleasant little city lying in the foothills of the Olympic Mountains, about sixty miles southwest of Thessalonica. Some time ago Dr. Dick Hillis and I had the privilege of standing on the steps of the synagogue where Paul preached in Berea. This ancient synagogue has been excavated, and the fact has been established that this was the actual synagogue in which Paul preached. We took great joy in standing on those steps and trying to preach to each other! Later I entered the evangelical church in Berea, and when I went to the pulpit and found the Greek Bible, I opened it to this very text:

Now these Jews were more noble than those in Thessalonica, for they received the word with all eagerness, examining the scriptures daily to see if these things were so.

Luke draws a sharp contrast between the rabble in Thessalonica—with their unthinking, prejudiced minds, and their emotional, impulsive actions—and these Jews in Berea, who were more noble. In what way were they noble? Their nobility was that they not only received the word but also checked it out with the Scriptures. A noble person is one who has both an open mind and a cautious heart.

The Scriptures are given to us as our guide, so that we can tell what is true and what is false, what is right and what is wrong. Unless a Christian uses these Scriptures, he is lost in a sea of relativism; his mind becomes confused and blinded, and he can be misled and easily manipulated, as the rabble manipulated the crowd in Thessalonica. These Jews, however, had the nobility to find out whether what Paul said was confirmed by the Scriptures.

The value of this story to us, and the reason Luke includes it, is that we might learn the necessity of testing any man's word. Don't listen to just one man's tapes, or read only one man's books or messages. This is a very dangerous practice. You will be misled by his errors and you won't know how to recognize them. Never give yourself to following a single man. Paul writes to the Corinthians, "You who do this are carnal. You follow

Apollos or Cephas or Paul, but we are all provided for your instruction. You need us all." Do not ever limit yourself to a single man's ministry, including mine. Establish what the Word of God says; that is the authority.

To Establish the Church

The account concludes with a very familiar pattern:

> But when the Jews of Thessalonica learned that the word of God was proclaimed by Paul at Beroea also, they came there too, stirring up and inciting the crowds. Then the brethren immediately sent Paul off on his way to the sea, but Silas and Timothy remained there. Those who conducted Paul brought him as far as Athens; and receiving a command for Silas and Timothy to come to him as soon as possible, they departed (Acts 17:13-15).

Here come the hounds of hell, panting down the road from Thessalonica. These Jews are not content to drive Paul out of Thessalonica; they pursue him for sixty miles, and when they arrive, they employ the same familiar tactics. They move in and stir up the thoughtless crowds, who in turn set upon Paul and Silas, so that poor Paul has to slip out of the city again by night. (It seems like Paul never left a city by daylight!) Now he is on his way by sea to Athens, leaving Silas and Timothy behind to establish the church.

And of course this is the point of the whole story. Paul is free to leave because he has left a church behind. God has implanted a believing community which will be a bridgehead in the midst of the evil of that city, arresting its corruption and dispelling its darkness as they operate in the freedom and liberty of the body of Christ. There may be a stiff battle for a while, but eventually the light will penetrate the darkness and men will be able to think straight and act righteously, even though they are not yet Christians. The light of the gospel lifts the whole level of community life. That is why Paul was so concerned that these young Christians left in Berea and Thessalonica would grow in grace, understanding the power committed to them and exercising it to set these communities free.

When I was in Berea I found that the church which Paul had implanted has now become the persecutor. The Spirit has had to break in afresh with a new body of believers who meet in secret places so as to avoid persecution and oppression. The Greek Orthodox Church, lineal successor to the church that Paul started in Greece, has now become sunken in apathy, liturgy, ritual, and dead orthodoxy, and is persecuting the fresh, alive, evangelical church of these areas. The church I visited was deliberately built behind a group of buildings in a little compound, where it could be partially hidden. The believers could not advertise their meetings and had to meet secretly, at unscheduled times. They could not openly evangelize within the city, but had to meet from house to house. Yet a very fruitful work was going on in these cities.

This should indicate to us that any group can become the instrument of evil as well as good if the life of the body in that group is not kept fresh and vital. When a group does lose its savor and its light, it becomes an instrument of evil and darkness. Then God has to awaken a new body, pouring new wine into new wineskins so that the freshness and vitality of the gospel will not be hindered.

> Finally, brethren, farewell. Mend your ways, heed my appeal, agree with one another, live in peace, and the God of love and peace will be with you. . . . The grace of the Lord Jesus Christ and the fellowship of the Holy Spirit be with you all (2 Cor. 13:11, 14).

CHAPTER EIGHT

ATHENS VERSUS PAUL

Acts 17:16-34

At the time of Paul's visit to Athens that city was no longer important as a political seat; Corinth was the commercial and political center of Greece under the Roman Caesars. But Athens was still the university center of the world. It was the heir of the great philosophers, the city of Pericles and Demosthenes, of Socrates, Plato, Aristotle, Sophocles, and Euripides—these men who established patterns of thought that have affected human learning for centuries. Almost all philosophies follow, in some degree, the teachings of these men. But Athens was long past its zenith when Paul visited it. It was now four hundred years after the golden age of Greece, and though Athens was still a center of art, beauty, culture, and knowledge, the city had lost all political importance.

Paul came down from Berea with certain unnamed Christians and was left alone in Athens. He sent word back to Silas and Timothy, whom he had left in Berea, to join him there. Evidently the apostle did not intend to stay long in Athens. He was heading for Corinth, for Paul always focused upon those centers of commerce where the influence of a church would be borne rapidly into the surrounding regions. He had decided to wait for Silas and Timothy in Athens, and Luke now tells us what happened there:

> Now while Paul was waiting for them at Athens, his
> spirit was provoked within him as he saw that the
> city was full of idols. So he argued in the synagogue
> with the Jews and the devout persons, and in the
> market place every day with those who chanced to
> be there. Some also of the Epicurean and Stoic
> philosophers met him (Acts 17:16-18).

This section is a powerful revelation of why the
gospel needs to be presented to every culture and every
age of the world. While Paul was waiting, he did what
any tourist does in Athens: he went sightseeing. Athens is
a striking city: it boasts the great temples of the
Acropolis, crowned by the Parthenon (now in a ruined
state but nevertheless still one of the most beautiful
buildings in all the world), as well as many other
theaters, temples, and marketplaces. As the apostle
walked around the city he saw the gods of Athens, the
idols that were being worshipped. According to one con-
temporary source, there were thirty thousand gods in
Athens at this time! Petronius, one of the ancient
historians, said that is was easier to find a god in Athens
than a man! Many of these statues have survived, and
copies of them are widely displayed as samples of ancient
art. But Paul recognized that these were not merely objects of art, but actually idols whom the people of Athens
worshipped.

Provoked to Preach

Luke tells us that Paul's spirit was provoked when he
saw this. The Greek word translated "provoked" is the
basis for our word "paroxysm." Paul's spirit was gripped

by an intense paroxysm, a storm within, as he saw the city given over to idolatry. Although the idols revealed that these men and women of Athens had a great capacity for God, each idol also revealed a distortion which sabotaged that capacity.

What Paul felt was very much akin to what must have moved a group of Christian students, some time ago, to run an ad in their university newspaper, from which this paragraph is taken:

> **Why are we Christians willing to follow Jesus into suffering in order to accomplish his mission of liberation? Because Jesus has changed our minds about a lot of things, and we can no longer tolerate the foolishness and futility that is passed out as wisdom at this university. We are tired of the "enlightenment" of this age which is blindly ignorant of its intellectual slavery to materialism and its contradictory obligation to ethical relativism. We are tired of seeing people's lives wasted and unfulfilled because of their submission to the established world order.**

That expresses exactly what the apostle felt as he moved about and saw the cloud of idolatry that hung over this city, blotting out the truth and plunging these people into the darkness of superstition.

So Paul began to preach. He could not help it; he knew that the only message that could help people in this state was the delivering word of Jesus. There were three groups to whom he spoke. First, he went into the synagogue and spoke to the religious people, the Jews and devout persons who were there. These Jews (and the Greeks who were following Judaism) were opposed to the idolatry of the city but could do nothing to prevent it.

They themselves were delivered from idolatry, but they were powerless to deliver the city because they were focusing on their own religious experience. To them Paul preached the gospel with seemingly little effect.

Then there were the common citizens of the city whom he met in the marketplace, the *agora* of ancient Greece—tradesmen, people going about their business, commercial people coming in with their wares to the city square. Here were people who were unthinking victims of the idolatry that held the city in its grip. They were sunken in superstition and gripped by fear, uncertainty, dread of darkness, and inner tensions and turmoil—all results of following false gods.

Atheists and Pantheists

Then there was a third group, the philosophers. Although these men were free from the crass idolatry of the city, they were offering the barren concepts of pagan philosophy as an alternative. Two kinds of philosophies are mentioned here, epicureanism and stoicism, and these same systems of thought are very much in evidence today. The Epicureans were atheists; they denied God's existence and a life after death. They were also materialists; they felt that since this life was the only thing that really existed, men should therefore get the most out of it. To them, pleasure was the highest virtue and pain was the greatest evil. Their motto (and it still persists to this day) was "Eat, drink, and be merry, for tomorrow we die." They were existentialists, living for the experience of the moment.

The Stoics, followers of the philosopher Zeno, were pantheists. They believed that everything is God and that he does not exist as a separate entity. Rather, he is in the rocks and trees and every material thing. Their attitude toward life was one of ultimate resignation, and they prided themselves on their ability to take whatever came. Their motto, in modern terms, was "Grin and bear it." Also, they taught moderation; they urged their followers not to become overemotional, either about tragedy or happiness. Apathy was regarded as the highest virtue of life. There are many people today who feel that the best thing they can do is to take whatever comes and handle it the best they can. They are proud fatalists, just as these Stoics were.

Contempt and Curiosity

Luke gives us the initial reaction of these two philosophical groups to Paul's teaching:

> And some said, "What would this babbler say?" [Those were the Epicureans.] Others said, "He seems to be a preacher of foreign divinities"— [because he preached Jesus and the resurrection. [These were the Stoics.] And they took hold of him and brought him to the Areopagus, saying, "May we know what this new teaching is which you present? For you bring some strange things to our ears; we wish to know therefore what these things mean." Now all the Athenians and the foreigners who lived there spent their time in nothing except telling or hearing something new (Acts 17:18-21).

The Epicureans, who were basically atheistic materialists, were contemptuous of what they heard from

Paul. They treated him with utter disdain. They said, "What would this babbler say?" The word "babbler" is literally "seed-pecker." They saw Paul as one of the little birds in the marketplace going around pecking at seeds here and there. They regarded him as a mere collector of fragments of truth, gathering a few choice words from philosophies that he had picked up along the way and trying to impress people. They smiled and dismissed him contemptuously.

The Stoics, however, were more interested. But Luke is careful to tell us that their interest did not arise out of a genuine desire to know and understand what Paul said, but out of a shallow curiosity. They were intrigued by the fact that he seemed to present two new gods, one named Jesus and the other named Resurrection. This was not an unusual concept for Athens; throughout the city you could find altars erected to various themes. There were altars to Shame, Reason, Virtue, and various other concepts. When they heard Paul speak of resurrection, they thought this was the name of a god and that he was preaching two new deities. They pricked up their ears because, as Luke said, "All they lived for was to hear something new."

Here in ancient Athens were all the classes of humanity that are still with us today. There were the religious oddballs, remote from life and powerless to affect it; there were the thoughtless idolators, sunken in superstition, living lives of quiet desperation, as do millions of people today; there were the atheistic existentialists; and there were the self-sufficient fatalists. To all these the apostle presented one thing—the delivering word of Jesus, the word of the power of God unto salvation.

In due course the people brought Paul before the

Areopagus. If you visit Athens today you will be taken up a small rocky hill without buildings, west of the Acropolis, and told that this is the Mars Hill where Paul addressed the Athenian philosophers. But although the word "Areopagus" does mean Mars Hill, it was also the name given to a court of judges who had the final authority in the city of Athens at this time. It is much more likely that it was this *court* before whom Paul was brought. They no longer met on Mars Hill, although they had originally done so. By this time they were probably meeting in one of the porches surrounding the marketplace. So it is before the court of the Areopagus that Paul appeared.

Point of Contact

In the message Paul gave to them we have a splendid example of just how the gospel operates to deliver men. He began with a most captivating introduction:

So Paul, standing in the middle of the Areopagus, said: "Men of Athens, I perceive that in every way you are very religious. For as I passed along, and observed the objects of your worship, I found also an altar with this inscription, 'To an unknown god.' What therefore you worship as unknown, this I proclaim to you" (Acts 17:22, 23).

A good introduction always begins where people are, and Paul began right where these Athenians were. He did not denounce them, he did not attack their idolatry; in fact, he paid them a compliment as far as he could. He said to them, "As I've been walking about your city, I've noticed one thing about you: you are a very religious people." The expression he used was literally "you are god-fearers." But the word he chose for "god" was rather unusual. Instead of the common word, *theos*, which means God in his greatness, he chose the word *daimon*, demon, by which he implied that the gods they worshipped were lesser concepts than the great idea of God. They understood that he meant to compliment them because they had a concept of and a capacity for God. They were very much involved with and interested in God.

Then he said he had come upon an altar to an unknown god. There were several of these in Athens. Many centuries before, a plague had been arrested by turning loose a flock of sheep within the city. Wherever the sheep were found they were slain and offered to a god. If they were slain near the altar of a recognized god they were dedicated to that god, but if they were slain apart from any of these, an altar was erected and dedicated to an unknown god! Paul found one of these and said, "This is the God I want to talk about. What you worship ignorantly I have come to declare to you." In this great introduction the emptiness of paganism is revealed. If you do not worship the true God, there is no end to your search; you will keep on going forever. The Athenians had thirty thousand gods, but even these were not enough; they had also erected altars to an *unknown* god! How clearly this voices the agony of humanity, the cry for a God they know exists but whom they cannot find.

Maker and Giver

In the rest of his message Paul first unfolds the truth about the living God which idolatry denied. Then he

shows them the corresponding truth about man, which
followed as a logical result of the truth about God:

**The God who made the world and everything in it,
being Lord of heaven and earth, does not live in
shrines made by man, nor is he served by human
hands, as though he needed anything, since he
himself gives to all men life and breath and
everything (Acts 17:24, 25).**

What he is saying here is that God is the *Maker* and not
the one who was made. God was not created by man; he
is the One who makes man and everything else that exists
in all the universe. He is the originator of all things.

We have not moved very far from ancient idolatry.
They used to take a piece of gold or silver or wood and
carve or form an idol, thus worshipping the works of
men's hands. Today we don't use images, but we still see
men worshipping themselves, projected to infinite
proportions. Man simply thinks of himself, projects this
into infinity, and worships that; that is his god—and that
is exactly what idolatry is. Paul points out that this is not
in line with reality. God is not the projection of man; God
is greater than man; he is the Maker, and not the made.

Second, God is the Giver, and does not have any
needs himself. "The God who made the world and
everything in it is not served by human hands as though
he needed anything, since he himself gives to all men life
and breath and everything." Idolatry and paganism
taught that men had to bring gifts to the gods, they had
to do things for their gods, to propitiate them and
sacrifice to them and bring them all kinds of things.
Today men are still doing the same thing. We are not

free from idolatry, for if a god is that which is the most important thing in a person's life, to which he gives his time and effort and energy, that which occupies the primary place of importance to him, then men have many gods even today. Money, fame, your children, yourself—all these and more can be your gods. You can even worship your country as your god. I am appalled at the number of people today who worship America and enthrone it as the highest value in life, the only thing for which they would give their lives, the only thing worth living for. These false gods make continual demands upon us; they do nothing for us, but we must work for them.

Paul cancels all this out. He says the real God is one who gives, who pours out. He does not need anything from you. He does not live in temples made by man. I'm sure Paul must have pointed to the Parthenon as he said this, for it was regarded as the home of Athene, the goddess for whom the city was named. God does not live in places like that, Paul said, and there is nothing you can give him that he needs. Rather, he is continually giving himself to you.

Seekers Are Rewarded

The third great truth was to show how God draws men and does not seek to evade them. To the pagans the gods dwelt on remote Mount Olympus. Men had to go through perilous and hazardous journeys in order to find and placate their gods, while the gods hid themselves from men. But Paul's message is that the true God is not doing that:

**And he made from one every nation of men to live on
all the face of the earth, having determined allotted
periods and the boundaries of their habitation, that
they should seek God, in the hope that they might
feel after him and find him (Acts 17:26, 27).**

The true God is the God of history. He made man as
one race, originating from one source. The interesting
thing is that today this statement is as scientifically sound
as when it was first uttered. Science today admits that
there is only one race of men, one species, Homo sapiens.
Despite the differences in skin color, body size, and facial
features that exist around the world there is only one race
of men. They all come from one source. Furthermore,
God has intervened to direct their lives throughout the
course of history. He has determined where they will live
and how long they will live there, as well as how long it
should take for a nation or an empire to rise and then fall
again—not arbitrarily, but based upon their reaction to
the one great reason for which human beings exist, that
they might find God, "that they might feel after him and
find him."

The events of human history have all served the one
great purpose that men might be motivated to search for
God. Hebrews 11:6 says, "For whoever would draw near
to God must believe that he exists and that he rewards
those who seek him." In Jeremiah 29:13, 14 we read,
"When you seek me with all your heart, I will be found
by you." God is urging men to seek him. That is why
catastrophes come, those tremendously difficult
events—in order to show men that they are not independent. It is ridiculous, absurd, and dishonest in the
extreme to think that we can operate without God. Our
very life and breath come from him continually.

Man Is Not Nothing

The apostle concludes his address with a wonderful statement about man:

Yet he is not far from each one of us, for
  "In him we live and move and have our being";
as even some of your poets have said,
  "For we are indeed his offspring."
Being then God's offspring, we ought not to think that the Deity is like gold, or silver, or stone, a representation by the art and imagination of man. The times of ignorance God overlooked, but now he commands all men everywhere to repent, because he has fixed a day on which he will judge the world in righteousness by a man whom he has appointed, and of this he has given assurance to all men by raising him from the dead (Acts 17:27-31).

Paul begins with the fact of the dignity of man, recognizing that man is God's offspring. It is not Biblical to go around telling people that man is nothing, that he is vile, that he is a worm. That is not the Biblical view of man as he was created. I sometimes hear Christians talking as though they were nothing and God is everything. Although I understand what they mean, the truth is that man is *not* a mere nothing. He can *do* nothing, but the Bible never says that he *is* nothing. What the Bible says is that man is the image of God, and that he has a capacity to respond to God. He is made for God.

Everywhere you go, even among the most degraded and primitive of men, you will find this pattern of the image of God. You will never find a man, woman, boy, or girl who does not have a passion for life, who does not want to live, who is not in revolt against death and boredom and frustration and all the other negative qualities of life. They all want to seize hold of life. And you will never find a man, woman, boy or girl who does not have a passion for dominion, who does not want to succeed, who does not want to reach out and try something new and accomplish new objectives, to conquer new territory. That is because man is made in the image of God. Further, you will never find a human being who does not have some power to create, to invent; some ability to produce or fashion or make or shape. This is inherent in the heart of man everywhere, and sets man apart and distinct from animals. These are all part of the image of God, and this image is man's greatest dignity.

But right along with this the apostle mentions the tragedy of man. "Being God's offspring [which even your pagan poets recognize is true], we ought not to think that the Deity is like gold, or silver, or stone, a representation by the art and imagination of man." He is saying that if it is true that we are made with a capacity for God, if we know that we are made to contain and reflect God, then it is not only insulting to God to make an idol of him, but it is also degrading to man. It is saying that we can be satisfied with things that are less than ourselves. Wherever people act on that basis, the result is that they return to childish actions. Idolatry of any kind makes a man act like an infant. In Edwin Markham's great poem, "The Man with the Hoe," as he is thinking of man in his low estate, he asks,

Is this the thing the Lord God made, and gave
To have dominion over sea and land,
To trace the stars, and search the heavens for power
And feel the passion of eternity?

Even in that degraded estate a capacity for God is recognizable. The tragedy is that this capacity is being prostituted into something less than the God for whom it was designed.

From Ignorance to Responsibility

The last thing Paul points out is man's responsibility. Men have lived, he says, in times of ignorance. Now these "times of ignorance" need to be understood carefully. This phrase does not refer to a certain date on the calendar. It is not speaking of Old Testament times as such, or of past dispensations before the present era. These "times of ignorance" are related only to the individual; they refer to the time in our lives when we, as the offspring of God, were trying to satisfy ourselves with things that were less than God. This is always a time of ignorance, when a man is operating on a level that reveals his utter ignorance of reality. Paul declares that God overlooks these times. He does not wipe us out. He does not judge us, he does not hate us and reject us, but he patiently waits while we live through these struggling times.

But the apostle further declares that when a man hears about Jesus, when he hears the good news that Jesus Christ is the way to the heart of God, he then has a responsibility before God to change his mind, to stop acting as he did before. That is what repentance means: a change of mind. You are responsible to change your mind and lay hold of that which God has provided in Jesus Christ.

Paul gives us here three great facts which underscore the importance of repentance. First, there is an *in-*

escapable day which God has fixed as the time when he will judge the world. Everyone knows this. A day is coming when our life will be laid open before everyone, and all the value of it, or its lack of value, will be evident. On that day every life will be evaluated. Second, there is an *unchallengeable Judge*. The One who will do the evaluating will not be a god, remote upon Mount Olympus, but he will be a Man, someone who has lived right here with us, who knows what human life is like, who has felt everything we feel. He will be the One who passes judgment on that day. Third, God has made this evident to all by an *irrefutable fact*: he raised that Man from the dead. On that fact Christianity ultimately rests. If you can disprove the resurrection of Jesus you can destroy Christianity in one blow. But as long as that fact remains unshaken, undestroyed, Christianity is indestructible. The fact that God raised Jesus from the dead is the guarantee that everything God says will happen will indeed take place.

Luke gives us, in these closing words, the reaction of Athens to Paul's message:

> **Now when they heard of the resurrection of the dead, some mocked; but others said, "We will hear you again about this." So Paul went out from among them. But some men joined him and believed, among them Dionysius the Areopagite and a woman named Damaris and others with them (Acts 17:32-34).**

Some mocked, which means their pride was threatened. Mocking is always the defense of pride when it feels itself attacked but has no logical defense; it resorts to ridicule. But Christianity ridiculed is always a sign of weakness, an admission of defeat. Some others delayed

their response, succumbing to the curse of the intellectual: academic detachment. They viewed themselves as
outside the system they were examining and thus
detached from it. "Everyone else is subject to this but
us." So they said, "We will listen to you again on this; we
need more evidence." Such are the delaying tactics
which many intellectuals are using today.

But some believed. That is the great word here. Some
repented, changed their minds. This indicates that
among these intellectuals were some earnest, honest people who were trying to find the answers to life. Such a
person was Dionysius the Areopagite. He was one of the
judges, an intellectual, a ruler of the city, but he became
a Christian, and with him was a woman named Damaris.
There were others among them, though we don't know
how many—perhaps just a few. Because it was a university city, Athens was much more resistant to the gospel
than any other city would be, but there were nevertheless
some who believed.

Here then is a church planted in Athens. We never
hear anything about it again, although I suspect that the
Letters to the Corinthians were also shared with the
church in Athens, because the cities were not very far
apart. Paul addresses the Corinthian Letters to "all those
who in every place call on the name of our Lord Jesus."
We do not know what happened to the church at Athens
except that here in the midst of this darkness the light of
Jesus Christ began to shine, and a body was formed.
From that body, power began to penetrate into the
secluded areas where evil sat entrenched, shaking men
loose and setting them free from the chains of darkness.

**Our Father, we pray for our own age, our own
generation, our own world. We know how men have**

pursued the emptiness of pagan philosophies in our day and how men are trying to satisfy the emptiness within with some lesser concept than you. They can never do so and are therefore rendered restless and unhappy, never finding what they are looking for. Others are resistant to this message, Lord, preening themselves in their intellectual pride, trying to find their own way by the power of reason. Father, we pray that everywhere this great message may have its effect as it did on Athens, and that our darkened society will be set free from its bondage to materialism and made to be what you intended us to be: warm, whole, balanced, happy, excited, and alive. We ask it in the name of Jesus Christ, Amen.

CHAPTER NINE

THE CROSS IN CORINTH

Acts 18:1-22

From Athens, the intellectual capital of the Roman world, the Apostle Paul now travels to Corinth, the center of sensuality. These two cities are symbols of the twin evils which, in every age and every generation, trap and enslave the hearts of people: intellectual pride and sensual lust.

Corinth is about fifty miles west of Athens, and when Paul visited the city it was the capital of the Roman province of Greece, which they called Achaia. It was a center of commerce and trade, located on a narrow neck of land between the Adriatic Sea and the Aegean Sea. The Greeks had built a skidway across that narrow isthmus, over which they actually dragged small ships on greased skids. Corinth was a magnificent city filled with beautiful temples of all kinds and located in a natural setting that I found breathtaking on my last visit there.

It was also the center of the worship of Aphrodite, the goddess of sex. There was a great temple of Aphrodite on the Acrocorinth, the hill in back of the city, and every evening a thousand priestesses of the temple would come down into the city streets to ply their trade as cult prostitutes, indulging in the worship of sex. Thus Corinth had gained a reputation throughout the whole Roman world as the center of sensuality. Whenever a citizen of

Corinth was portrayed in a drama, he would be a morally loose character, and usually a drunk. This is the city to which the apostle came, walking all alone in the dust of the road.

Corinth was infested with certain stubborn strongholds of evil which the apostle describes in his First Letter to the Corinthians. Sexual license and perversion were rampant. Racial discord was prominent. There were family feuds and political tyranny. And of course spreading over everything was the emptiness and lack of purpose which paganism always produces. Corinth was so very much like our own cities! We live in Corinthian conditions today, and if there is any church in the New Testament with which we could particularly identify, this is the one.

Paul arrived in Corinth a total stranger; he had never been there before, and he knew no one. But he was confident that God would open the door.

> After this he left Athens and went to Corinth. And he found a Jew named Aquila, a native of Pontus, lately come from Italy with his wife Priscilla, because Claudius had commanded all the Jews to leave Rome. And he went to see them: and because he was of the same trade he stayed with them, and they worked, for by trade they were tentmakers. And he argued in the synagogue every sabbath, and persuaded Jews and Greeks (Acts 18:1-4).

Paul always expected God to lead him to someone who would open the door to a city, and in Corinth (probably in the marketplace) he ran into a fellow Jew who, like himself, was a tentmaker. This was Aquila, who with his wife, Priscilla, had just been driven out of Rome by the decree of Emperor Claudius. Paul and Aquila began to work together, and, as you can well imagine, it was not very long before Paul led Aquila and Priscilla to Christ. These two are frequently mentioned in the pages of Scripture as faithful workers and helpers of the apostle.

Notice, in passing, that Paul led them to Christ while he was at work. I hope this will encourage you to use your work as a place for getting to know people, getting to understand their needs, and as a normal place for evangelism—but not on company time. Work is an excellent place to make contacts with people who are searching for answers in life.

Kicked Next Door

Now when Silas and Timothy rejoined the apostle, arriving from Thessalonica, Paul altered his procedure. We read,

> When Silas and Timothy arrived from Macedonia, Paul was occupied with preaching, testifying to the Jews that the Christ was Jesus. And when they opposed and reviled him, he shook out his garments and said to them, "Your blood be upon your heads! I am innocent. From now on I will go to the Gentiles." And he left there and went to the house of a man named Titius Justus, a worshiper of God; his house was next door to the synagogue. Crispus, the ruler of the synagogue, believed in the Lord, together with all his household; and many of the Corinthians hearing Paul believed and were baptized (Acts 18:5-8).

Here is the account of a great period of success in the opening weeks at Corinth. Paul taught in the Jewish synagogue, and as usual it was not very long until the preaching of a crucified Christ aroused the hatred and the enmity of these Jews. In his Letter to the Corinthians, Paul speaks of the fact that the word of the cross is to the Jews a stumbling block. It aroused such enmity that they opposed him and reviled him, openly attacking him and sneering at him.

Finally Paul shook his garments against them in the Jewish gesture of detachment and said, "If you will not receive this message I will go to the Gentiles." (This applied only to Corinth, because in the next place Paul visited he started in the synagogue again.) But he didn't go very far; in fact, he went right next door. It is clear from the Greek text that the house of Titius Justus and the synagogue actually shared a common wall. So Paul still had access to the synagogue, and the first thing we read about after his move is that Crispus, the ruler of the synagogue, was won to Christ. He believed in the Lord, together with all his household. Also, among the other citizens of Corinth there was a tremendous response; many who heard Paul believed and were baptized.

Although some people claim that Paul did not believe in baptism, it is important to note that everywhere he went his converts were always baptized. As he says in his Letter to these Corinthians, he did not very often baptize himself because he didn't want people bragging that the apostle had baptized them. But obviously Silas and Timothy helped him, and all of these converts were baptized.

Fear and Trembling

The next section of this account reveals the inside

story of Paul's reaction to the city of Corinth, which is very interesting:

> **And the Lord said to Paul one night in a vision, "Do not be afraid, but speak and do not be silent; for I am with you, and no man shall attack you to harm you; for I have many people in this city." And he stayed a year and six months, teaching the word of God among them (Acts 18:9-11).**

What the Lord literally said when he appeared to Paul in this night vision was, "Stop being afraid, but keep right on speaking." This reveals that Paul was indeed becoming afraid. It is quite understandable that he would, for a very familiar pattern was developing. He had seen it before many times. He had come to the synagogue and spoken to the Jews. They had rejected his message. He turned to the Gentiles and there was immediate response, a great flood of people coming in. This aroused the anger and hostility of the Jews, and Paul knew that the next step was Trouble, spelled with a capital T. He anticipated that he would soon be ousted from the city by either the aroused rabble or the authorities.

Paul's fear is so beautifully descriptive of the humanity of this man! We usually think of Paul as being bold and fearless, yet he suffered just as we do from apprehensions, forebodings, and fears. In fact, in First Corinthians 2 he says, "When I came to you . . . I was with you in weakness and in much fear and trembling. . . ." He was very much afraid of what would happen to him in Corinth. The entrenched powers of darkness were being shaken, and the life of the city was being disrupted by the awakening which was spreading because of Paul's teaching.

But this is the only legitimate mark of the success of a church. Many churches today measure their success by what is going on in the congregation. It is wonderful to have things happening within the congregation, but that is not the mark of success. The church is successful only when things start happening in the city. The Lord Jesus said, "You are the salt of the earth . . . you are the light of the world." It is the world that God is aiming at. Until something starts happening in the community, the church is a failure. It bothers me greatly to come into a city and find it filled with church buildings on every side, but to find that the city is locked into patterns of violence and hatred, riot and bloodshed. It tells me that there is something seriously wrong with the churches of that city, for God always aims at the world, breaking down the patterns of evil that lock men and women in bondage. As the apostle saw this beginning to happen he knew he was in for trouble.

This is why the Lord appeared to his apostle. How gracious and reassuring are his words! He says, in effect, "Paul, don't let your fears grip you! Stop being afraid and don't keep silent. Keep right on preaching, because I am going to protect you. No one is going to set upon you and hurt you, for I have a lot of work for you to do yet in this city. There are many people here who haven't come to me yet, but they will—if you keep on preaching."

Pocket of Protection

I remember thinking one time when I read these words that a football quarterback is protected in this same way. His teammates form a pocket around him and the quarterback drops back into the pocket. There he is protected so that he can continue the assault. That is exactly what the Lord is saying to Paul. "Paul, don't worry. You see the hostility, you see the opposition, you see it all coming, but I have built a pocket around you. You just keep on throwing that ball."

Some of the Lord's most encouraging words are these: "I have yet many people in this city." They were still pagans, they had not yet become Christians—but the Lord knew they were there. There is nothing more encouraging to me in going into any strange situation than to realize that there are people there whom God already knows will respond to what I say. This gives me a great deal of support in preaching the truth. So it was with the apostle. He was greatly strengthened, and for a year-and-a-half he continued in Corinth without being molested. He was able to preach the truth until there was a great stirring in this city. The church at Corinth became a large church, with a powerful effect upon the life of the city.

It was also during this period that Paul wrote his First and Second Letters to the Thessalonians, perhaps the earliest of Paul's letters that we have in our Bible. Paul undoubtedly wrote to other churches during this time, for the New Testament mentions other letters which have not been preserved. But the Thessalonian Letters were preserved because they contain the full-orbed teaching of the New Covenant, which is essential for us to know.

When the attack against Paul finally does come, God's hand is still in control of the situation.

But when Gallio was proconsul of Achaia, the Jews made a united attack upon Paul and brought him before the tribunal, saying, "This man is persuading

men to worship God contrary to the law." But when
Paul was about to open his mouth, Gallio said to the
Jews, "If it were a matter of wrongdoing or vicious
crime, I should have reason to bear with you, O
Jews; but since it is a matter of questions about
words and names and your own law, see to it
yourselves; I refuse to be a judge of these things."
And he drove them from the tribunal. And they all
seized Sosthenes, the ruler of the synagogue, and
beat him in front of the tribunal. But Gallio paid no
attention to this (Acts 18:12-17).

This tribunal has been excavated, and you can see it if
you visit Corinth. It is called in Greek the *bema*, the
scale—that is, the judgment seat. When I was there I
walked around in the bema and tried to visualize the
apostle standing in front of this well-known prosecutor
and judge of Rome. Gallio is mentioned several times in
the historical accounts of that day. He was the older
brother of the philosopher Seneca, who at this very time
was busy tutoring the young Nero—who would become
the next emperor after Claudius. Gallio was said to be a
very just man, with a gracious and mild disposition. Here
he appears to be very impartial.

The charge brought against Paul by these Jews was
that he was violating the Roman law against beginning a
new religion. "This man is persuading men to worship
God contrary to the law." They did not mean the Jewish
law; they meant the Roman law. Evidently these Jews
supported their charged with arguments concerning
Paul's preaching of Christ. But Gallio was a very astute
individual who furnishes us an example of how God often
uses governmental authorities to preserve the peace and
to permit the gospel to go forth. Before Paul could open
his mouth to defend himself, the judge threw the case

out of court. He refused jurisdiction. He said to the Jews,
"Look, if this man had committed a crime or had done
something wrong, I would judge him. But it is obvious to
me that all you are talking about are some silly semantic
distinctions between your own Jewish religious factions.
Therefore it has nothing to do with Roman law."

Freedom to Preach

That was a very important decision! It meant that
Paul was now free to preach the gospel throughout the
Roman empire without being charged with breaking the
Roman law. Gallio, in effect, said that Christianity, in the
eyes of the Romans, was officially a Jewish sect—it was a
part of Judaism. And Judaism was an established, official religion within the empire. This decision is what
made it possible for Paul to preach in many Roman cities
without any difficulty with the officials.

The Jews were so upset by this outcome that they
seized their leader, Sosthenes, and beat him up in front
of the tribunal, venting their spite on him. When Crispus
became a Christian he was no longer the ruler of the synagogue, so Sosthenes took his place and led the attack
against Paul. But when he mismanaged the affair so
badly that the whole thing was thrown out of court, the
Jews beat him right in the presence of the Roman judge.
All this left Gallio quite unconcerned. (The King James
Version says that the *Greeks* beat Sosthenes, but this
reading is not supported by the best manuscripts.)

That beating did Sosthenes a lot of good. In the First
Epistle of Paul to the Corinthians you will find a most interesting item in the very first verse:

> Paul, called by the will of God to be an apostle of Christ Jesus, and our brother *Sosthenes*. . . .

I would never consider beating as a method of Christian evangelism, but it certainly worked in this case! Evidently Sosthenes' eyes were opened when these Jews turned against him, and he decided that maybe their cause was not so just after all. He gave heed to the gospel and became a colaborer with Paul in spreading the gospel of Jesus Christ. All this is a beautiful picture of how God stands behind the scenes watching over his own. Do you remember that poem of James Russell Lowell?

> Truth forever on the scaffold.
>   Wrong forever on the throne.
> Yet that scaffold sways the future,
>   and behind the dim unknown
> Standeth God amid the shadows,
>   keeping watch above his own.

This was characteristic of Paul's ministry during these days!

Paul's second missionary journey now comes to an end right where it began, in Antioch:

> After this Paul stayed many days longer, and then took leave of the brethren and sailed for Syria, and with him Priscilla and Aquila. At Cenchreae he cut his hair, for he had a vow. And they came to Ephesus, and he left them there; but he himself went into the synagogue and argued with the Jews. When they asked him to stay for a longer period, he declined; but on taking leave of them he said, "I will return to you if God wills," and he set sail from

**Ephesus. When he had landed at Caesarea, he went
up and greeted the church, and then went down to
Antioch (Acts 18:18-22).**

Several things are worthy of notice in this paragraph.
Paul stayed in Corinth a long time after Gallio dismissed
his case. The Christian faith was now legally accepted, so
he had an open door and he used it to the full, preaching
there for perhaps as long as two full years. At last he took
leave of the brethren and, taking Priscilla and Aquila
with him, he sailed from Cenchreae, one of the ports of
Corinth.

We have the interesting comment from Luke that
there "he cut his hair, for he had a vow." The kind of
vow this refers to is a religious vow; according to the law
this was a way of expressing thanks. He had vowed that
for thirty days he would not cut his hair but would give
thanks to God and worship him. He probably fasted during this period as well, refraining from certain foods. At
the end of the thirty days he cut his hair, having fulfilled
his vow. It was simply a Jewish way of giving thanks.

Some are disturbed by this, thinking it means that
Paul was reverting to all the old, legalistic practices of
Judaism. But that is not the case at all; he was simply
doing as he described in a letter to the Corinthians: "To
the Jews I became a Jew; to the Gentiles . . . a Gentile."
Since he was working with the Jewish community, he
expressed in this Jewish way the thankfulness of his heart
for God's protection over him while he was at Corinth. It
was a perfectly proper thing for him to do. It does not
mean that when Paul came to the Gentiles he was not
perfectly free to lay aside all Jewish ritual and to live as a
Gentile. Paul was a man set free in Christ.

The voyage of Paul, Priscilla, and Aquila brought

them to Ephesus in the Roman province of Asia. Earlier, Paul had been forbidden by the Spirit to preach the word of the Lord in Ephesus, but now he was allowed to come in, although he stayed only a brief time. As usual, he began at the synagogue. They received his message and asked him to stay longer, but he was in a hurry to get back to Jerusalem. So, the account says, he left Aquila and Priscilla and went on, landing on the coast of Palestine at Caesarea and "Going up to greet the church," i.e., the church at Jerusalem. He spent some time there (we don't know how much), doubtless reporting on what God had done. Finally he came back to the church at Antioch, from which he had begun his journey some two or three years earlier.

Power Pattern

What has God been saying to us in the account of this missionary journey of Paul? Over and over again we have seen the pattern which these early Christians invariably followed whenever they came into a new city. From this form of approach God always brought a new and creative program designed to meet the specific needs of the situation there. One of the things this has taught me is that we make a great mistake by taking one fixed program and trying to apply it to every situation. According to the New Testament the early Christians always began with the preaching of the Word. Then, as it won people to Christ, they began to have body life—loving one another, praying for one another, understanding their spiritual gifts, and putting them to work. As the body of Christ began to operate, the rich and varied innovations of the Holy Spirit came into play and adapted the body and its activities to the specific situation. Thus the Word went out with great power and began to shake up the surrounding community within a relatively short period of time.

We need desperately to return to this pattern today, and I believe God is moving the church back in this direction. I hope we learn once and for all the lesson of this section of Acts: God is prepared to work to bring down the strongholds of evil, to shake up a city, to shake up a neighborhood, and to set men free.

Think these things through and ask yourself, "Have I found my spiritual gift, and am I ministering with it as a member of the Body of Christ? Am I part of the moving of the body of Christ in this area, to accomplish what God wants done?"

Our heavenly Father, we thank you for this account which encourages us, for we know that you are at work today just as you were then. This same sense of electric excitement can grasp and grip us as it did these early Christians. This same mighty power can be turned loose in communities that are in the grip of strongholds of darkness and evil, and these strongholds can be broken apart. The forces of evil can become demoralized in our area as the body of Christ begins to function. Lord, help us who are members of that body to take due note of where we are, and what we are doing, and whether we are fulfilling the task committed to us by the Lord Jesus when he gave us spiritual gifts and the power of his resurrection, so that we may be working members of this body. We ask in Jesus' name, Amen.

CHAPTER TEN

HALFWAY CHRISTIANS
Acts 18:23—19:7

The Apostle Paul enjoyed a short but well-deserved rest in Antioch after being on the road for two to three years. But, as Luke tells us, he didn't rest for long:

> **After spending some time there he departed and went from place to place through the region of Galatia and Phrygia, strengthening all the disciples (Acts 18:23).**

On his third missionary journey the apostle started out all alone; he had no Barnabas or Silas with him this time. But he was heading out to familiar ground, to minister among dear friends whom he personally had led to Christ. His purpose was to strengthen the churches. Paul loved to venture into new territories, but he never forgot the need to strengthen those already won; he devoted this third journey to the strengthening of his converts.

This meant that Paul's ministry among the churches in Galatia and Phrygia was to teach them the Word of God, for it is the Word that strengthens. In his Letter to the Galatians Paul recalls that he came among the believers telling them the truth. Jesus also, in his high-priestly prayer recorded in John 17, says to the Father concerning his disciples, "Sanctify them in the truth; thy

word is truth." This is what builds Christians up—the
knowledge of the Word of God, and obedience to that
Word! The Word is the instrument which produces
maturity. You cannot grow as a Christian without a continually increasing understanding of the Word. Furthermore, there is no chance for effective evangelism without laying the groundwork of maturity. Although any
Christian can witness from the very day he is born again,
there can be no effective, continuing evangelism without the spiritual growth which involves maturing in the
understanding of the Scriptures. So the apostle went
back to the churches to teach them the Word of God.

The next section is a parenthesis which Luke inserts
in this account of Paul's ministry to explain what
happened when Paul finally reached Ephesus, and to in-
troduce us to Apollos. This story continues into the opening section of Chapter 19, so we will disregard the
chapter division.

> Now a Jew named Apollos, a native of Alexandria,
> came to Ephesus. He was an eloquent man, well
> versed in the scriptures. He had been instructed in
> the way of the Lord; and being fervent in spirit, he
> spoke and taught accurately the things concerning
> Jesus, though he knew only the baptism of John
> (Acts 18:24, 25).

This golden-voiced orator of the first century was not
yet a Christian at this time; he was a Jew who had been
trained in the Jewish schools at Alexandria in Egypt. He
had become a powerful speaker, well versed in the
Scriptures—literally "mighty" in the Scriptures. But of
course he could go only to the limit of his own knowledge
and understanding. No preacher can ever lift his con-

gregation above his own spiritual experience. Apollos knew only the baptism of John, which was a great deal, for it was the truth about Jesus—but it was not the whole truth.

Wilderness Witness

This term "the baptism of John" means the message which John preached. When John the Baptist went out into the wilderness of Judea and began to preach (about six months before our Lord appeared), the inhabitants of Jerusalem and the cities of Judea went out into the desert to hear him. This mighty preacher did not come to them—they went to him, indicating that his message was a startling one for his day. To us, who have the full presentation of Christianity, John's message does not seem particularly striking. But to the people of his day it hit like a sledgehammer.

Basically John declared three great truths: first, he announced that forgiveness of sins is possible before God only on the basis of repentance. Thus there was no real value in a sacrifice or offering. These Jews had been taught that the only way they could have their sins forgiven was by means of an animal substitute whose blood was shed on their behalf. Thereby God passed over their sins by accepting, at least temporarily, the blood of the animal on their behalf, thus forgiving their sins. But John came with the startling word that what God really wanted was a repentant heart.

John had the people express their repentance in baptism, which was a symbolic act of cleansing. This too was something new. In the Old Testament you can read in the law about certain cleansings which were to follow a sacrifice. These were similar to baptism, but not quite the same. John was announcing that as people repented, changing their mind about their sin and calling it what God called it and forsaking it, then God forgave their sins. The symbol of that forgiveness was the washing of baptism. John insisted that their repentance must be real, and that they actually produce fruit that befitted repentance. That is, their actions had to demonstrate that they really meant what they said and would indeed turn from their evil. John met several different groups of people and told them specific things that they could do in order to indicate that they had really judged themselves before God.

Third, John announced that One was coming who would complete the work he had begun. Repentance is just a beginning with God. It is as far as we human beings can go by ourselves, but it does not give us life. Repentance would achieve forgiveness of sins, but it would not give any positive ground of action, any power by which to live. That is what John announced would be available when Jesus came. "There is coming one after me," he said, "who is mightier than I, whose shoes I am not worthy to carry. I have baptized you with water, as a symbol of the forgiveness God gives. But he will go further; he will baptize you with the Holy Spirit. He will put life into you, and give you power to live as God asks. That I cannot do."

So Apollos knew this much, but he knew nothing of the cross or of the resurrection, and he did not know of the coming of the Holy Spirit on the day of Pentecost. His message was basically incomplete. He announced the word about Jesus but said nothing about the three essentials which make it possible for the power of Jesus to be experienced in our life: his death, his resurrection, and the coming of the Holy Spirit. Luke now records what happened next:

> He began to speak boldly in the synagogue; but when Priscilla and Aquila heard him, they took him and expounded to him the way of God more accurately. And when he wished to cross to Achaia, the brethren encouraged him, and wrote to the disciples to receive him. When he arrived, he greatly helped those who through grace had believed, for he powerfully confuted the Jews in public, showing by the scriptures that the Christ was Jesus (Acts 18:26-28).

Aquila and Priscilla were Christians, so it is interesting to note that they still met on the sabbath day with the Jews in the synagogue. They undoubtedly also had Christian meetings in their home (probably on Sunday, the first day of the week, the day of resurrection), but here they are in the synagogue, where they hear Apollos preach Jesus. He preached the things concerning Jesus very accurately, Luke tells us, and they were warmed and expectant because of this, but they soon learned that there was something missing.

So they did a beautiful thing—they invited the preacher home to dinner with them and helped him with his problem. I don't know whom to admire more in this situation, Aquila and Priscilla, or Apollos. These two dear Christians, not too old in the Lord themselves (having been led to Christ by Paul in Corinth), do not scorn this young man for his incomplete preaching. They do not write letters to the editor about him, or reject him or criticize him, but instead they invite him home and lovingly and wisely expound to him the more accurate presentation of Christ. This means that they showed him how the Old Testament Scriptures indicated the death and resurrection of Christ and the coming of the Holy Spirit. They expounded to him so that his faith would rest not merely upon their testimony of the historic occurrences but also on the predictions of the Old Testament.

Teachable Teacher

But I really don't know if they were greater in all this than Apollos, who was willing to sit under the teaching of members of his congregation and listen humbly to them. What amazing news it must have been to Apollos that the message of John had now been fulfilled, that the One whom John had baptized had gone on to fulfill all that God had ever predicted concerning the way of salvation for men. The implications of the cross, the resurrection, and the coming of the Holy Spirit were all explained to Apollos.

Naturally he needed time to digest these facts and to rethink everything. There is no indication here that he immediately began to preach this new truth at Ephesus. Rather, he desired to go over to Corinth, probably because there was a congregation of believers there who had been instructed by the Apostle Paul. Aquila and Priscilla, his teachers, had been led to Christ by Paul in Corinth, and so Apollos wanted to go where he could learn more about what he had heard. The brethren in Ephesus sent letters of recommendation with him so that the brethren in Corinth would receive him.

Apollos was a great help to the Corinthian brethren when he came. Here was a man who knew the Old Testament Scriptures. "When he arrived, he greatly helped those who through grace had believed," doing what he could do best, answering the arguments of the Jews right in public, proving from the Scriptures that Jesus was the Christ. And how much more could he do this now, armed with the new facts he had learned about the Lord Jesus! In his First Letter to the Corinthians Paul acknowledges the fact that he had planted, but Apollos had watered. Paul was grateful for the ministry of this mighty man of the Scriptures who could confirm and strengthen the word that Paul had planted there.

Now Paul appears again:

While Apollos was at Corinth, Paul passed through the upper country and came to Ephesus. There he found some disciples. And he said to them, "Did you receive the Holy Spirit when you believed?" And they said, "No, we have never even heard that there is a Holy Spirit." And he said, "Into what then were you baptized?" They said, "Into John's baptism" (Acts 19:1-3).

After visiting the churches of Galatia and Phrygia, Paul came to Ephesus, just as he had promised at the close of his second journey. You remember that Luke tells us:

And they came to Ephesus, and he left them [Priscilla and Aquila] there; but he himself went into the synagogue and argued with the Jews. When they asked him to stay for a longer period, he declined; but on taking leave of them he said, "I will return to you if God will," and he set sail from Ephesus (Acts 18:19-21).

Now Paul is fulfilling his promise by returning to Ephesus. Naturally he went to the synagogue where he had been invited to stay, and when he came into the

Jewish community he found certain disciples. We are not told whose disciples they were, but it is clear from the previous account that these were disciples of Apollos. They were men and women whom Apollos had told about Jesus, at least to the extent of the baptism of John. Paul heard them speaking about Jesus, and he obviously thought they were Christians when he first met them. But as he watched them he observed that something was missing, and I'm sure there was puzzlement in his voice when he finally said to them, "Did you receive the Holy Spirit when you believed?"

This question indicates that the normal Christian pattern is that the Spirit is given immediately upon belief in Jesus Christ. There is no suggestion here that the Spirit of God is given after a long period of belief in Christ. Jesus himself had predicted that the giving would be immediate. In the seventh chapter of John we are told that on the great day of the feast Jesus stood up and proclaimed, "If any one thirst, let him come to me and drink. He who believes in me, as the scripture has said, 'Out of his heart shall flow rivers of living water.' " John adds, "Now this he said about the Spirit, which those who believed in him were to receive . . ." (John 7:37-39). So it is *belief in Jesus* which brings the Holy Spirit.

These people whom Paul met in Ephesus knew something about Jesus. They appeared to be disciples of Jesus, but something was missing. What it was we are not told. Perhaps Paul saw that there was no joy in their lives, or no peace or certainty. Certainly there was no power. They were still under the domain of the law and had not yet been delivered into the joy and peace of the full Christian message. So he asked them, "Did you receive the Spirit when you believed?"

The disciples answered that they had never even

heard that there is a Holy Spirit. This does not mean that they never knew of the third Person in the Trinity, for John clearly taught the doctrine of the Holy Spirit. The Holy Spirit had come upon Jesus when John baptized him, and John knew this. They meant, "We have never heard that the Holy Spirit is now given, that he has come, as John announced that he would." Paul, understanding that, asks them, "What were you baptized into?" And they replied, "Into John's baptism." It was immediately clear to Paul what the problem was—they were halfway Christians. They had come as far as repentance and forgiveness of sins, but they knew nothing about the work of the Holy Spirit. So he begins to instruct them:

And Paul said, "John baptized with the baptism of repentance, telling the people to believe in the one who was to come after him, that is, Jesus." On hearing this, they were baptized in the name of the Lord Jesus. And when Paul had laid his hands upon them, the Holy Spirit came on them; and they spoke with tongues and prophesied. There were about twelve of them in all (Acts 19:4-7).

Paul undoubtedly gave them full instruction in the truth about Jesus, which Luke simply gathers up in these brief phrases. Paul went on to tell them about the death of Jesus, and what that accomplished with respect to the old life they had been living; and then about the resurrection which made available to them a risen life, a different kind of life; and then about the coming of the Holy Spirit, who would make all this real in their experience continuously, moment by moment, day after day.

A Second Baptism

After Paul instructed these Ephesian believers in this way they were rebaptized in the name of Jesus. This is very significant, for it indicates that the baptism which they had received with an incomplete knowledge of Jesus was really not Christian baptism. I meet many people who have been baptized as babies, when they had no opportunity to understand what the Christian message was all about and no opportunity to exercise faith in a risen Lord who could indwell them and strengthen them by his Spirit. Sometimes they ask me, "Do you think I should be rebaptized, now that I have really come to know a risen Lord?" On the basis of this text I say to them, "Yes, you should, because your baptism did not represent your personal faith in a risen, abiding Lord."

When these people came to this understanding they were rebaptized by the Apostle Paul, who laid his hands upon them. Please understand that he did not impart anything to them; that is never what the laying on of hands does. Rather, it signifies *identification*. Paul is identifying these twelve people with the body of Christ, that new body formed by the Holy Spirit when he came on the day of Pentecost. By laying his hands on them he is signifying their union with the family of the Lord Jesus. The moment Paul performed this act of identification the Spirit came upon them, actually joining them to the body of Christ. They believed on Jesus and the unifying Spirit came immediately.

Two Gifts

The mark of the Spirit's coming was the impartation

of spiritual gifts. It is strange to me how often people read this passage and note only that they spoke in tongues. They immediately think that this is another Pentecost. But there are *two* gifts mentioned here. Whenever the Holy Spirit comes he always gives spiritual *gifts*. He did so when he came into your life, and the whole aim and purpose of your redemption is to discover and put to work those spiritual gifts which were given to you. And here, when the Spirit came, they began immediately to exercise two spiritual gifts, the first of which was speaking in tongues. This is listed as one of the gifts of the Spirit in First Corinthians 12. It is very natural that this gift would be given on this particular occasion, for, as Paul tells us in First Corinthians 14, the gift of tongues is designed especially as a witness to unbelieving Jews.

These twelve disciples were Jews. They had sat under the teaching of Apollos, probably having heard him in the synagogue at Ephesus. They lived in the Jewish community and were regarded as a sect or group of Jews. Now they have become Christians, but their friends and those all around them are still Jews. Within this setting (if not actually in the synagogue, then in the Jewish community), as they are now filled with the Holy Spirit they use the gift of tongues, in which they praise God in languages they had never learned. They do so publicly (never privately) as a sign to unbelievers that God is at work.

Remember that Paul tells us in First Corinthians 14 that this is the fulfillment of the prediction of the prophet Isaiah. Isaiah had said to the people of Israel in his day, "By men of strange tongues and by the lips of foreigners will I speak to *this people*, and even then they will not listen to me, says the Lord." That is, "When you see and hear men coming to you speaking with other tongues, then you will know that the hour has struck when God turns from Israel to the Gentile world. The gospel is now to go out to the Gentiles as well." This was the sign, then, to the unbelieving Jews. This is the Biblical gift of tongues, and it was perfectly proper that it should be exercised on this occasion, for this is the situation in which it was designed to be used.

Today there is an imitation gift of tongues, a psychological phenomenon which has been known among men for centuries. Even Plato discusses it in some of his lectures to the Greeks in Athens, four hundred years before Christ. It is a phenomenon frequently heard among all kinds and classes of people, but it does not measure up to the Biblical gift. Those who fall into it by mistake are misled, entering eventually into a time of real weakness in faith in which they are spiritually derailed for a while, until God in grace delivers them and sets them free to begin to grow again in faith in the Lord.

I fully understand the appeal that this makes to many Christians. It seems to offer such a wonderful experience and a shortcut to spirituality. It seems so desirable. I went through this very experience myself in my early Christian life, so I am well aware of its attraction. But as you compare it with the Biblical description of the gift of tongues, it is not the same thing. The Biblical gift is a proper one which will bless, encourage, and strengthen those who employ it. The false gift, however, leads only to spiritual blindness.

Along with the gift of tongues at Ephesus was also given the gift of prophesying. This is the ability to open and expound the Scriptures in power and truth. The word "prophet" comes from a compound Greek word: *pro-phaino. Phaino* means "to cause to shine" or "to make shine," and *pro* means "before." So a prophet is one who stands before the Word of God and causes it to shine, who illuminates people's lives with the power and truth of the Scriptures. Peter uses it that way: "We have a more sure word of *prophecy*, which shines as a light in a dark place." These twelve new Christians of Ephesus began to prophecy as the Spirit illumined their minds. They saw great truth in the Scriptures and began to declare it in power.

Note that one of these gifts was designed for unbelievers and the other for believers. The gift of tongues, Paul says in First Corinthians 14, is for unbelievers, but the gift of prophecy is for believers. Here in the community in Ephesus both groups were present: the unbelieving Jews who still refused to accept the truth of the Scriptures about Jesus, and those who had become Christians, who with Priscilla and Aquila were rejoicing in all that the Lord had given them and who needed this exercise of the gift of prophecy.

When these twelve people were filled, and the Holy Spirit had come upon them, they demonstrated this fact by their expression of these gifts of the Spirit. No apostle would ever again need to ask them, "Did you receive the Holy Spirit when you believed?" There was a difference about their lives. They obviously were now filled with new power and strength which came when they believed in Jesus.

There are many people today who believe in Jesus and yet do not show much evidence of the work of the Holy Spirit. In many churches where I am privileged to speak I have wanted to say to the people, "Did you receive the Holy Spirit when you believed?" Recently I was at a Christian college and spoke in chapel. As in most Christian colleges, though I found a wonderful group of fine, growing young Christians on campus, the chapel service was so dull and dead that I could hardly bear it. I sat on the platform looking out at this sea of sterility before me and thought to myself (I had been working on this text), "If the Apostle Paul were here I think he would stand up and say, with puzzlement in his voice, 'Did you receive the Holy Spirit when you believed?'" Yet they told me that the chapel services were much better than they had been!

Spirit of Expectancy

The Holy Spirit is given upon the exercise of belief in the Lord Jesus. This does not stop with one act of believing, and this is where we tend to get confused. We are to *keep on* believing in the Lord Jesus and to manifest his power and vitality in our lives. It is this continual act of believing which releases the freshness of the Spirit in our lives. Paul says to the Colossians, "As you received Christ Jesus the Lord, so live ye in him. . . ." As you received him by an act of believing, keep on believing and walking and living in him, so that you might demonstrate the power of the Holy Spirit. This is why, when some Jews came to Jesus and asked, "What must we do to do the works of God?" he answered, "This is the work of God, that you keep on believing in him whom he has sent."

So what is wrong if, in our Christian lives, there is no evidence of the working of the Holy Spirit, none of the joy, none of the grace, none of the power? It is because we are not believing in him. We believed in him once, maybe twenty or thirty years ago, but that believing has ceased. There is now no sense of expectancy, no fresh anticipation of his working in our lives *today*.

If I asked you, "Do you believe in Jesus?" you would probably say "Yes." Then I might ask, "Well, did you receive the Holy Spirit when you believed? Are the signs of the Spirit of God in your life? Are his presence, his power, his working, his freshness, his vitality, his enthusiasm, his excitement visible in your Christian life?" If not, you have ceased believing in Jesus. He makes himself available to us continually, moment by moment, to fulfill every demand which life makes upon us *if we expect him to do so.* This note of expectancy is the evidence or sign of faith which marks the difference between the sterility of religiosity without the Spirit, and the freshness and power of a Spirit-filled life. Paul's question addressed to those halfway Christians of long-ago Ephesus still has meaning for us today as we understand the need for a continual act of faith in the Lord Jesus.

> Lord Jesus, how frequently we fail to understand the truth of your promise to us that you have come to live within us, and that your life can be as visible in us today as it ever was in this first-century time. Grant to us anew, Lord, the faith to lay hold of this promise and to make visible in our lives, moment by moment, this same sweet freshness and sovereign moving of the Holy Spirit. Flame of God, we ask you to touch us, to burn away the dross and to set us afire with that which manifests the character and the life of the Lord Jesus. We ask in his name, Amen.

CHAPTER ELEVEN

DOWN WITH WITCHCRAFT!

Acts 19:8-20

The major problem in Ephesus was that it was a center for witchcraft. Superstition, demonism, and witchcraft held this city in its thrall. A weird mixture of black arts, worship of demons, astrology, and occult practices of various kinds had filled this city with priests, magicians, witches, warlocks, and quacks of every description. The inevitable consequence, as always among people who are held in bondage by witchcraft, was that people lived in fear and darkness, indulging their lusts in wicked, degrading practices, and were sunken in slavery, squalor, and drunken debauchery. Here indeed was a stronghold of darkness which could only be overcome by the weapons of truth and love and righteousness and faith—the weapons of *our* warfare.

Darkness Challenged

In this account we have another example of what can happen when a church begins to operate on the power that God has put at its disposal and functions in the way it was intended to function. Paul begins, as always, in the synagogue, as Luke tells us in verse 8:

And he entered the synagogue and for three months spoke boldly, arguing and pleading about the kingdom of God; but when some were stubborn and disbelieved, speaking evil of the Way before the congregation, he withdrew from them, taking the disciples with him, and argued daily in the hall of Tyrannus. This continued for two years, so that all the residents of Asia heard the word of the Lord, both Jews and Greeks.

And God did extraordinary miracles by the hands of Paul, so that handkerchiefs or aprons were carried away from his body to the sick, and diseases left them and the evil spirits came out of them (Acts 19:8-12).

What a remarkable account! Paul began, as he always did, with the weapon of truth. He spoke in the synagogue concerning the kingdom of God, which had come with the coming of Jesus Christ. This kingdom was opposed to the rule of Satan, the powers of darkness which reigned in human affairs. Human history is the checkered account of man's struggles to be free from that from which he cannot free himself. It is this rule of darkness, this authority of the kingdom of Satan, which the kingdom of God in Christ challenges. This is what Paul was preaching in the synagogue.

The Jews here had made Paul welcome and had invited him to come back. He had returned as he promised, and for three months, on every sabbath day, he reasoned with them out of the Scriptures about the kingdom of God. But when some of the Jews understood that to submit to the rule and authority of the Lordship of Jesus involved confessing the emptiness of their religious respectability, they opposed Paul. When they realized that they had to acknowledge that inwardly they were just as desperately dark and evil as anyone else, they resisted him.

So these Jews made trouble for Paul, as they always did, and at last he decided to withdraw, taking the disciples with him. They moved out of the synagogue into rented quarters, the hall of Tyrannus. This unquestionably was one of the lecture rooms which the Greek teachers employed to teach philosophy and various other subjects of the arts and culture of the day. Paul rented it, according to some ancient authorities, from eleven o'clock in the morning till four in the afternoon. The Revised Standard Version has a marginal note which says, "Other ancient authorities add, 'from the fifth hour to the tenth,' " which, according to the Greek method of reckoning, was from eleven till four o'clock.

That was the time in Ephesus when all the people were taking a siesta. They closed up their shops, went home and had a leisurely meal, took a nap, worked around the garden, etc. The working day began at about seven in the morning. The shops closed at eleven and everyone went home until four, when the shops reopened and business went on until about nine-thirty at night. This was their normal day. Evidently the Apostle Paul made tents during the morning hours to support himself. But at eleven o'clock he came to the hall of Tyrannus and lectured for five hours every day for two years.

Relay Evangelism

Five hours a day, six days a week, fifty-two weeks a year for two years adds up to 3120 hours of lecturing.

This equals 130 days of lecturing continuously for twenty-four hours a day. The content of those lectures was the great truths that we find in the epistles of Paul. Imagine the tremendous impact of this teaching! No wonder we read in verse 10 that "all the residents of Asia heard the word of the Lord, both Jews and Greeks." That was an entire province, an area larger than the state of California, filled with many cities.

Of course it was not Paul himself who was teaching throughout this area. It was the Christians who heard him in the lecture hall of Tyrannus and who, captivated and galvanized by these truths, began to spread the word throughout the whole area. They formed churches in other cities, which evangelized in turn, so that in two years this whole province was reached by the gospel of Christ.

It was during this time that the church of Colosse was begun by Epaphras and Philemon, who carried the gospel up the Lycus Valley into the cities there. Others, perhaps Trophimus and Tychicus, young men from this province, were involved in preaching to other cities of the region. They may have been the founders of the churches to which John later wrote his letters in the Book of Revelation—Smyrna, Sardis, Thyatira, Pergamum, Philadelphia, and Laodicea. All of these cities are in this area and were begun by these Christians, largely unnamed and unknown, who heard the Apostle Paul proclaiming this fantastically revolutionary truth in the hall of Tyrannus in Ephesus. What power there is in the Word of God!

In addition, Luke tells us, the word was confirmed by signs:

And God did extraordinary miracles by the hands of

Paul, so that handkerchiefs or aprons were carried away from his body to the sick, and diseases left them and the evil spirits came out of them.

Underline the word *"extraordinary."* These miracles were unusual, of a different kind than previous miracles. What made them unusual was that they were performed by carrying away these cloths from the body of Paul, so that the miracles were accomplished at a distance from him.

No Magic in Sweatbands

There is nothing magic about this! There was no value inherent in the cloth. In fact, we can be misled greatly by the translation here. It was very difficult for the translators to put this word in terms that would be meaningful to us in the Western world, for these were not handkerchiefs or aprons in the usual sense. They were not little cloths that Paul used for blowing his nose nor aprons that ladies wear in the kitchen.

The "handkerchiefs" were literally sweatbands, strips of cloth which Paul bound around his head as he worked at making tents, to keep the sweat from running down into his eyes. They were, therefore, associated with the labor, the toil, that he went through to make the gospel available. The aprons were made of leather, and he wore them while making tents, not while fixing his meals. It was these that were used for these miracles. Again, this is not an attempt to support the practice of many faith healers of today who anoint cloths and mail them around the country. That is superstition, hocus pocus, a form of magic. That is not what Luke is talking about at all.

These are *symbols* which God chose to employ in order to underscore the characteristic of the apostle which made him a channel of the power of God, in the same way that Moses' rod was a symbol. Cast on the ground, the rod became a serpent; lifted over the waters, it rolled them back. There was nothing magic about the rod itself; it was the *symbol* of something about Moses which God honored. So these sweatbands and trade aprons were symbols of the honest, dignified labor of the apostle, his labor of love and humility of heart, his servant-character which manifested and released the power of God. God means to teach by this that it is through a man whose heart is so utterly committed that he is ready to invest hard, diligent labor in making the gospel available, willing to stoop to a lowly trade, that the power of God is released.

Satan on the Bandwagon

The first sign of the crumbling of the stronghold of darkness in Ephesus was the attempt on the part of the powers of darkness to make an alliance with the Christian cause. As we have seen before, this is one of Satan's favorite tricks. He tries to join the team:

> Then some of the itinerant Jewish exorcists under-took to pronounce the name of the Lord Jesus over those who had evil spirits, saying, "I adjure you by the Jesus whom Paul preaches." Seven sons of a Jewish high priest named Sceva were doing this. But the evil spirit answered them, "Jesus I know, and Paul I know; but who are you?" And the man in

whom the evil spirit was leaped on them, mastered all of them, and overpowered them, so that they fled out of that house naked and wounded. And this became known to all residents of Ephesus, both Jews and Greeks; and fear fell upon them all; and the name of the Lord Jesus was extolled (Acts 19:13-17).

These seven sons of Sceva knew a good thing when they saw it. They were sons of a Jewish high priest, and they recognized that here was an opportunity to use religion, and the widespread interest in religion, to advance their own cause. So they attempted to jump on the bandwagon and, employing these two names as though they were some kind of magic formula, they tried to cast out evil spirits by saying, "I adjure you by the Jesus whom Paul preaches."

This reveals something remarkable about people of this kind. We have many like them today, fortune-tellers and swamis and yogis and gurus and mediums. They know enough about the occult to sound impressive, but basically they are ignorant dupes, fooling around with powers they do not understand, and who have little control over what will happen when they become involved with such powers.

Evil Routed by Evil

But what happened here in Ephesus was almost ludicrous. As Sceva's sons adjured the evil spirit by these names, the man in whom the evil spirit dwelt (notice Luke's careful distinction, as a physician, between the man and the evil spirit who possessed him) was under the control of that spirit. The spirit seized him and empowered him to challenge these seven sons and to take them all on singlehanded. You can imagine the scene as they tumbled out of doors and windows with their clothes torn half off, bloody and wounded, driven out by this possessed man.

The evil spirit was angered by this use of the name of Jesus because his authority was threatened, and what he said in response to this adjuration is interesting. He used two different words for "know." He said, "Jesus I know" (using a word that means "I know him with a deep, instinctive, innate knowledge") and "Paul I am acquainted with" (i.e., "I know his name, I know who he is; I don't know him as well as I know Jesus, but I am acquainted with him") but "Who are you?" That was the signal for his attack upon them, resulting in their ridiculous exodus. This incident, no doubt because of the humor involved, became known all over Ephesus, with both Jews and Greeks hearing about it. It *was* impressive. And the result was that the name of Jesus was magnified. These people of Ephesus were impressed because here was a name of power—power in the realm of the invisible world.

This is also the first sign of a crack in the stronghold of darkness that held the city in thralldom. As Jesus said, "When Satan's kingdom is divided he can no longer stand." Here you see a kingdom divided. These Jewish exorcists, who were the unwitting dupes of satanic philosophy, were attacked by an evil spirit who supposedly should have been on their side. Already the kingdom is beginning to crumble under the attack of truth and love and righteousness and faith, these weapons of the Christians' warfare.

The $10,000 Bonfire

This combined assault went on to yield a tremendous degree of success. Luke now gives us the next scene:

> Many also of those who were now believers came, confessing and divulging their practices. And a number of those who practiced magic arts brought their books together and burned them in the sight of all; and they counted the value of them and found it came to fifty thousand pieces of silver. So the word of God grew and prevailed mightily (Acts 19:18-20).

There were two movements in this development. It started with the believers, the Christians, who began to clean up their own lives, who came and divulged their hidden practices, confessing what they were doing in private. Obviously these were relatively new Christians, who perhaps had never thought anything was wrong with these practices. But as they sat under the teaching of the apostle, and saw the kingdom of God and how God longs to set people free, they began to see that what they had been doing—the astrology, the reliance on horoscopes, the belief in the influence of the stars, and all their other superstitious practices—had held them in bondage. Because of these practices they were weak and fearful, upset and distressed within themselves. So they began to confess all this and thus become freed from their bondage.

This in turn precipitated another movement. The pagans around them in the city began to take a second look at their own practices. Many of them who had practiced magic arts brought their books together and burned them when they became Christians under the influence and power of the gospel, and thus they were set free from their deadly delusion. This is a beautiful illustration of how light breaks forth through the church, which is the light of the world. When the church begins to clean up its own life, then the world will begin to see itself as it is and be moved to start straightening up and becoming free.

These people surrendered all their occult literature, and that was a costly thing to do. As they totaled up the value of these books and the various paraphernalia that were brought to be burned, it came to fifty thousand pieces of silver. This is approximately ten thousand dollars, which was a tremendous sum in those days. It meant that these people were forsaking their livelihood. They were actually changing the total pattern of their lives as they saw that they could no longer practice the occult and live as Christians. It revealed how willing they were to be free from this terrible practice.

The Weapon of His Warfare

This account makes very clear the means by which witchcraft seizes hold of people. Human beings are not easily invaded by demonic force. God has made man to be a king, and has built into us certain safeguards which operate naturally to keep us independent, free from control by these demonic forces which are supernatural and present all around us. They cannot force their way into a human life. They cannot simply overpower us and take possession, though they long to do so. What they must do, therefore, is deceive us. They must find a way by which they can trick us into yielding our wills to their influence and power. And when we voluntarily give way, then they move in, possess the mind, control the thoughts, and dominate the whole life.

This was very sharply called to my attention a few years ago when I was teaching a home Bible class. Among those attending were a number of people who had been involved with witchcraft, scientology, and various other practices of this type. A girl took me aside after a class was over and said, "I want to ask you about something. I've been having some strange experiences. They started about a year-and-a-half ago when I was a schoolteacher in Alaska. Another girl and I roomed together, and during those long winter evenings, when there was nothing to do, we whiled away the time by amusing ourselves with a Ouija board. We were getting various answers and messages by doing this and we thought of it as nothing but a game.

"But soon I began to be aware of very strange thoughts in my mind when I'd go to bed at night. I would seem to think of certain words and strange things to say. At first I could put them out of my mind and go to sleep. But gradually they became more and more insistent, until I finally found that I couldn't sleep unless I'd pay attention to them and think about them. Then these inner voices began to suggest that I take a pencil and write these things down. At first I tried to resist, but they became more and more insistent and I found that I couldn't go to sleep until I'd write down what they told me. It was always filthy, obscene words.

"Then I talked with my roommate and found that she was going through the same experience. Shortly after that we came down here to California. Now I can't go to sleep until I write out, sometimes for hours at a time, all the filthy things which these voices insist that I say. Now," she said, "is this God?"

I said, "No, you are becoming the victim of the powers of darkness." I turned to Deuteronomy and showed her what the Word of God said there, warning the people of God against these things which are an abomination to the Lord. She was tremendously helped by this. Then I showed her how to become a Christian, and she received the Lord. I told her to pray and ask God for help whenever she felt this kind of influence. Several weeks later I saw her in a restaurant and she said, "It's been so marvelous to be free from those voices. I've been doing what you suggested whenever they approach and I'm finding that the Lord keeps them away."

This whole business of astrology and horoscopes, of Ouija boards and of scientology, of yoga and other practices of Eastern philosophy—these are all means by which satanic forces trick us into opening our minds and yielding our wills to them. The books on any of these subjects, if you read them, all suggest that you are going to discover a "hidden" power that few people know about. A man writes me almost every week about some new book he has found in the back room of some obscure bookstore, covered with dust and hidden in the back shelves, and which, he has now discovered, contains the secrets of the universe. "Such tremendous truths it contains!" He says that if I would just read one of these books my eyes would be opened and I'd learn and understand so much that I don't know now. The trouble is that I do not see that he knows any more than I do . . . or

even as much. But this is the way these evil powers attempt to seize upon us.

Here in Ephesus Paul and the other Christians, by the power of the truth, broke through this deception. They assaulted this stronghold of evil and cracked it wide open, so that Luke says, "The word of the Lord grew and prevailed mightily."

That is how a church ought to operate—in the power of the Spirit, and by the authority of the Word. There are strongholds like this all around us today, bastions of darkness. Drugs is one, witchcraft another, homosexuality a third. There are a hundred thousand homosexuals in San Francisco alone, deluded and trapped by a philosophy which urges them to accept their condition and treat it as though it were normal and natural. This will lock them into a bondage they will never be freed from. How desperately this situation needs the assault of truth and of light, as does the whole matter of crime, terrorism, and revolution. God longs to deliver people from these strongholds, and he has given the church this power.

Our heavenly Father, we thank you for the truth that is revealed here. We see similar powers of darkness holding people enthralled today, locking them into misery and heartache, superstition and fear, hostility and emptiness. Lord, help us to understand that this is a very strategic time to live, and that we must not waste our time, frittering it away in empty activity. Help us to give ourselves to this exciting, glorious encounter against these powers of darkness. We ask it in Christ's name, Amen.

CHAPTER TWELVE

CHRISTIANITY IS DANGEROUS

Acts 19:21—20:1

A most descriptive definition of a Christian is that he is completely fearless, continually cheerful, and constantly in trouble! Surely nothing could better describe the Apostle Paul in his ministry to the world of his day. He was—by faith, not by nature—completely fearless, continually cheerful, and certainly constantly in trouble. This indicates an inherent quality of Christian life. Christianity is a very dangerous faith. We are followers of One who said, "I have not come to bring peace on earth but a sword, and to make a division among men" (Matt. 10:34 paraphrased). By that seemingly paradoxical means Christ purposes to heal the warring of earth, to repair the brokenness of mankind, and to join men into one great body, sharing life together.

When Paul came to Ephesus he found the sordid powers of evil entrenched in a stronghold over the city, holding it in bondage. Paul attacked that stronghold with the most powerful weapons ever known, and within two years it was demolished.

It looked then as if Paul's work there were over, as if the Marines had landed and the situation was well in hand. So the apostle evidently began to think of moving on.

Now after these events Paul resolved in the Spirit to pass through Macedonia and Achaia and go to Jerusalem, saying, "After I have been there, I must also see Rome." And having sent into Macedonia two of his helpers, Timothy and Erastus, he himself stayed in Asia for a while (Acts 19:21, 22).

At this time three things occupied the apostle's heart and moved him to take this action. First was that which he said weighed upon him daily: the care of the new Christians who had come to Christ in Macedonia and Greece—in Thessalonica and Berea and Philippi, in Athens and Corinth. He longed to impart more truth to them so that they might learn how to live their lives in the power of the Holy Spirit.

The second thing that moved Paul was an intense desire to penetrate to the very center of the Roman empire and culture with the claims of Christ, to plant the gospel in the fullness of its power in the very capital, in Rome itself. "After I've been to Jerusalem," he said, "I must see Rome." Dr. G. Campbell Morgan says, "That's not the 'must' of the tourist; that's the 'must' of the missionary." He longed to help the Christians who were already there and to instruct them. On the very journey which he will soon commence, when he comes to Corinth, he will take time to write his great Epistle to these Roman Christians, so as to help them even though he is hindered from getting there. But he also determines that at last he will come to Rome.

Hungry Saints

The third thing, merely suggested here by Luke, is the concern and desire in his heart to help the famine-stricken saints of the church at Jerusalem. Already a great famine had descended upon the land of Judea. The Christians in Jerusalem were hungry, and Paul longed to help them. So he sent Timothy and Erastus into Macedonia. Here we are not told why, but from one of Paul's letters we learn that Timothy and Erastus were sent to tell the churches there about the need of the Christians in Jerusalem, and to collect an offering for them in advance. Then, when the apostle came he could send it or take it to Jerusalem. We can read this in Paul's First Letter to the Corinthians:

> **Now concerning the contribution for the saints: as I directed the churches of Galatia, so you also are to do. On the first day of every week, each of you is to put something aside and store it up, as he may prosper, so that contributions need not be made when I come. And when I arrive, I will send those whom you accredit by letter to carry your gift to Jerusalem. If it seems advisable that I should go also, they will accompany me (1 Cor. 16:1-4).**

He reminds these Corinthians,

> **I will visit you after passing through Macedonia, for I intend to pass through Macedonia, and perhaps I will stay with you or even spend the winter, so that you may speed me on my journey, wherever I go. For I do not want to see you now just in passing; I hope to spend some time with you, if the Lord permits. But I will stay in Ephesus until Pentecost, for a wide door for effective work has opened to me, and there are many adversaries (1 Cor. 16:5-9).**

It was the apostle's plan to stay in Ephesus until the day

of Pentecost, but his mind was soon changed. Luke tells us now in Acts 19 what caused him to alter these plans:

> About that time there arose no little stir concerning the Way. For a man named Demetrius, a silversmith, who made silver shrines of Artemis, brought no little business to the craftsmen. These he gathered together, with the workmen of like occupation, and said, "Men, you know that from this business we have our wealth. And you see and hear that not only at Ephesus but almost throughout all Asia this Paul has persuaded and turned away a considerable company of people, saying that gods made with hands are not gods. And there is danger not only that this trade of ours may come into disrepute but also that the temple of the great goddess Artemis may count for nothing, and that she may even be deposed from her magnificence, she whom all Asia and the world worship" (Acts 19:23-27).

The silversmiths at Ephesus had been organized into a trade union. And they found that they were being hit hard in the most sensitive part of the human anatomy: the pocketbook. I heard a man say the other day that he saw a friend looking very gloomy. He asked his friend, "What's the matter?" The friend said, "My wife has just made me a millionaire." He said, "Well, what's wrong with that?" The friend answered, "I used to be a multimillionaire!" Anything that hits us in the financial area always strikes home!

He Saw Red (Ink)

These silversmiths, who made little silver souvenirs of

the goddess Artemis, found their business tremendously diminished because so many people were becoming Christians that nobody wanted their idols anymore. Demetrius, the president of the union, cared nothing for the real welfare of the hundreds who had become Christians and had found freedom and peace and joy in Christ. He saw only the red ink in the profit-and-loss columns of his books, and he was very concerned about that. It is interesting that archeologists have found in the ruins of Ephesus an inscription bearing the name of the man Demetrius.

The problem was, of course, that the vested interests in Ephesus were being threatened. In our day, many have charged that the war in Vietnam continued for so long simply because there are men in this country who have vested interests in making money by means of the military machine. There is a certain degree of justification for this charge, because there have always been profiteers who care nothing for the fact that lives are lost and bodies smashed and mutilated, so long as they make a fast buck. Profiteering is nothing new.

There is a profound revelation of mob psychology in the account Luke gives us. For, after all, you cannot arouse a mob to defend your interests if all you can say is that you haven't been making as much profit as you used to. That may interest *you*, but it doesn't interest other people. They don't care whether you make any money or not. The lack of revenue was what stirred up these silver-smiths, but since no one would defend them on this basis, Demetrius had to add another charge, deliberately introduced and emotionally loaded, in order to arouse the citizenry.

The charge was that the religion of the city was being threatened—that Artemis, the goddess the city worshipped, was being insulted by this loss of income and was in danger of losing her stature in the eyes of the world. Artemis, the goddess whose temple was known as one of the seven great wonders of the world, was apparently fashioned from a meteorite, because later on the town clerk reminds the people of the "sacred stone" that had fallen from the sky. According to some of the copies that have been excavated she was the figure of a many-breasted woman, enshrined as the goddess representing Mother. In attacking Artemis the Christians were attacking Mother, and when you attack Mother and apple pie, you are really striking to the heart of a deep emotional issue! These riot engineers in Ephesus well knew that they could stir up the whole city with this issue, for this was the season of the year when Ephesus gave itself over to a whole month of feasting, revelry, and debauchery centering on the worship of Artemis. They called this festival the "Artemision." It had the characteristics of the Mardis Gras in New Orleans, and the city was packed with people who had come for this special occasion.

Unfounded Charges

There are two very interesting and revealing things about this speech by Demetrius. First, he was evidently quite unaware of how ridiculous his charge really sounded. If Artemis was so great that the whole world worshipped her, then why was she not able to defend herself against this attack? If her power was so great that she commanded the worship of men, why did she need the support of the city of Ephesus to defend her? No one ever seems to face this kind of question when raising such an issue.

Second, Demetrius was obviously blind to the significance of the way by which his trade had been ruined. It had not been openly attacked by Christians. Paul had never said a thing against the religion of Ephesus. He had never denounced the temple and had in no way tried to attack this pagan superstition. In fact, the town clerk will openly admit that "These were not blasphemers of the goddess, nor robbers of the temple."

Now this is most interesting; there was nothing negative about their approach. These early Christians did not go around faulting paganism; rather, they introduced a positive new faith of such tremendous power and such fantastic reality that, when anyone experienced it, the old way of life was wiped out. The old was devitalized by the appearance of the new, and there was no need for attack. The Christians simply declared Jesus Christ and his availability to man. And men and women lost in darkness and superstition and gripped by fear found him so loving, so genuine, so joyful that all their empty paganism grew pale by comparison. It never seems to have dawned upon Demetrius that this was what had happened and that therefore there was no possible way of defending against it. If the Christians had attacked this pagan philosophy, then a defense could have been erected. But they said nothing about it. It was simply "the expulsive power of a new affection," to use Thomas Chalmers' marvelous term.

Assembly of Confusion

Luke continues his account of the mob and its actions in verse 28:

When they heard this they were enraged, and cried

out, "Great is Artemis of the Ephesians!" So the city was filled with the confusion; and they rushed together into the theater, dragging with them Gaius and Aristarchus, Macedonians who were Paul's companions in travel. Paul wished to go in among the crowd, but the disciples would not let him; some of the Asiarchs also, who were friends of his, sent to him and begged him not to venture into the theater. Now some cried one thing, some another; for the assembly was in confusion, and most of them did not know why they had come together (Acts 19:28-32).

That sounds familiar, doesn't it? How little human nature has changed in two thousand years! Here was a crowd, excited by a false emotional issue, which surged together into the theater. If you visit the site in Ephesus today you will find that this theater has been excavated. It is the only sizable part of the city which still stands. It was a huge theater, able to seat about twenty thousand people, so this was a vast crowd. These people were very responsive to this appeal, although there were many who did not know what it was all about.

Paul wanted to go in and speak to them. What an insight into the fearless bravery of this man of God, who did not hesitate a moment to take on a crowd like this! But his friends recognized that the mood of the crowd was ugly. Even the Asiarchs, the political rulers of the province of Asia who were responsible to the Romans, were concerned and sent word to Paul not to venture into the theater. That is very revealing. Paul had made friends among these rulers, who understood and were impressed by the message of Christ. Though Luke does not say they were Christians, they were nevertheless favorably inclined and tried to protect Paul from this wild and raging mob.

Luke then goes on to show how impossible it would have been for Paul to do anything to quiet them:

Some of the crowd prompted Alexander, whom the Jews had put forward. And Alexander motioned with his hand, wishing to make a defense to the people. But when they recognized that he was a Jew, for about two hours they all with one voice cried out, "Great is Artemis of the Ephesians!" (Acts 19:33, 34)

Here is a wild mob that has no argument other than simply to chant, over and over again, this slogan which aroused their pride and fed their egos and ministered to their emotions. The Jews were very concerned, doubtless because they had lived in this city for many years and were known to be opposed to the worship of idols. They had a synagogue there and had made it clear that they were not idol worshippers and did not approve the practice, but the Jews had no effect upon the populace. They stood for the right cause, but without any power to affect others. Nevertheless, they were afraid they might be implicated in this disturbance and so they prompted Alexander, one of their number, to stand up and explain their attitude and to make clear that they were not the ones who had affected the business of selling idols.

This is very likely the same Alexander to whom Paul refers in his Letter to Timothy. Timothy had become, by the time Paul wrote, a bishop of the church at Ephesus. Paul wrote, "Beware of Alexander the coppersmith, who did me great harm." I remember years ago hearing a Baptist preacher comment on this text. He said that he too had been damaged by Alexander the coppersmith, as he looked at the collection plate and saw all the pennies there!

But the crowd refuses to hear Alexander and drowns out his words with a chant which continues for more than two hours, over and over monotonously, "Great is Artemis of the Ephesians!" When a crowd gets to the point where its emotions have been so aroused that its reasoning power is lost, it is in a very dangerous state. These Asiarchs were quite correct in their concern for the apostle because, with but the slightest suggestion, this crowd could have been sent raging through the streets, demolishing everything in its path.

No Need to Shout

The mob was finally quieted by the town clerk, whose office in those Greek cities corresponded to that of mayor. Luke tells us what happened:

And when the town clerk had quieted the crowd, he said, "Men of Ephesus, what man is there who does not know that the city of the Ephesians is temple keeper of the great Artemis, and of the sacred stone that fell from the sky? Seeing then that these things cannot be contradicted, you ought to be quiet and do nothing rash. For you have brought these men here who are neither sacrilegious nor blasphemers of our goddess. If therefore Demetrius and the craftsmen with him have a complaint against any one, the courts are open, and there are proconsuls; let them bring charges against one another. But if you seek anything further, it shall be settled in the regular assembly. For we are in danger of being charged with rioting today, there being no cause that we can give to justify this commotion." And when he had said this, he dismissed the assembly (Acts 19:35-41).

This town clerk, whose name is not given to us, is an admirable politician and orator. He intervenes at precisely the right psychological moment. The crowd, having exhausted itself with its senseless roaring of the slogan for two hours now, is ready to listen at last. So he stands up to speak, setting forth three logical points. First he says, "Yes, Artemis is great; therefore there is no need to shout. We can count on her to defend herself, so why worry? Nobody is going to be able to overthrow a goddess as great as ours, so we don't need all this commotion."

Second, "The men that you are charging have really done nothing provocative. They have not blasphemed the goddess; no such charge has been brought against them. They have not robbed the temple, nor been sacrilegious in any way. The courts are open, and if that doesn't satisfy you, the legislature is available. The normal channels of protest are open to you, so why don't you use them? Third, "We are seriously in danger of losing the freedom of this city as a result of this indiscretion." For he well knew that the Romans would tolerate anything except civil disorder. If an unexplained riot occurred they were in danger of losing their status as a free city, unencumbered by direct Roman rule.

This is the telling point. You can see that this town clerk has nothing more in mind than that which would normally concern a politician—keeping the peace. He really doesn't care about the issues; he doesn't want to examine them. He only wants to keep everything orderly, so he puts a suppressing hand upon the unruliness. This is the way men think. Yet in all this God was overruling the wildness of this mob, calming the emotional passions which were surging in the hearts of so many people and were creating this uncontrollable situation. God quieted all this through the use of govern-mental channels.

In the opening verse of Chapter 20, after another of these unbelievably misplaced chapter divisions, you have the final sentence of the story:

After the uproar ceased, Paul sent for the disciples and having exhorted them took leave of them and departed for Macedonia (Acts 20:1).

Paul is anxious to explain this whole affair to the Christians. There is something about it he doesn't want them to miss, so he calls them together and exhorts them before he leaves.

To Make Us Rely on God

Luke doesn't tell us what Paul's exhortation consisted of, but I believe Paul himself does. There is a passage in his Second Letter to the Corinthians which refers to this very occasion. Some scholars doubt it, but in my judgment this is clearly a reference to this occasion. Paul says:

For we do not want you to be ignorant, brethren, of the affliction we experienced in Asia; for we were so utterly, unbearably crushed that we despaired of life itself (2 Cor. 1:8).

Imagine yourself with the apostle in the midst of this tremendous uproar. It was a very threatening circum-stance. It had appeared for awhile that the gospel had so triumphed in Ephesus that Paul could think of leaving and going on to other places. Then this riot suddenly occurred, seeming to threaten the entire cause of Christ and putting the Christians in great jeopardy and danger. Paul was crushed and very distressed. In fact, he said his very life was in danger. This crowd was so wild, so uncontrollable, that for a few hours it looked as though they might just sweep through the city and wipe out every Christian in Ephesus. Paul expresses it in these terms:

> . . . we were so utterly, unbearably crushed that we despaired of life itself. Why, we felt that we had received the sentence of death . . . (2 Cor. 1:8b, 9a).

Paul could not see any way out. It looked as if he had reached the end of the road.

> . . . but that was to make us rely not on ourselves but on God who raises the dead . . . (2 Cor. 1:9b).

This is the very heart of the Christian message, as Paul will go on to explain in the Corinthian Letter. "Our sufficiency is not of ourselves," he says. "It is not as though anything is coming from us; our sufficiency is from God. God alone is able. God without anything else, without reckoning on any human resources, is able." His explanation to these young converts in Ephesus was unquestionably along this line. He was saying to them, "God has sent this event, has allowed it to happen, in order to teach us that he is able to handle things when they get far beyond the resources to which we ordinarily look. God is able. And he has taught us this so that we will not rely on ourselves but upon him who raises the dead, who works in us to do exceedingly abundantly above all that we could ask or think according to the power at work within us."

He goes on in Corinthians to refer to this deliverance:

> ... he delivered us from so deadly a peril, and he
> will deliver us; on him we have set our hope that he
> will deliver us again. You also must help us by
> prayer, so that many will give thanks on our behalf
> for the blessing granted us in answer to many prayers
> (2 Cor. 1:10, 11).

What an awareness this apostle had of the fantastic
strength of the body of Christ working together, praying
together, supporting one another, upholding each other
in prayer and thus calling into action the mighty power
of the God of resurrection! He is the God who can work
through the most unexpected instruments to quiet a
situation, to hold a crowd in restraint, to stop the surging
emotionalism of people whose reasoning has been short-
circuited, to hold them within limits and bounds, and to
bring the whole affair to nothing! This is the might of our
God.

This is what Paul particularly wants us to learn from
this situation, as we too come into times of danger
and pressure and trouble. The difficulties which strike
suddenly in our lives, the pressures through which we
must go, the sudden catastrophes that come roaring in
unexpectedly out of the blue—these are sent in order
that we might rely not on ourselves but on God, who
raises the dead. So Paul sent for the disciples, and, having exhorted them, he took leave of them and departed
for Macedonia.

> Father, thank you for this reminder. We live in days
> very much like these, when human emotions can
> rapidly get out of control, when demonic powers

seem to rise suddenly and sweep through whole communities, affecting people far beyond what might be expected. Lord, these are dangerous times in which we live. We pray that we might not be so fatuous as to think that we are going to return to the quiet and peace of a time long past. But grant that we may be ready, Lord—confident, even eager, knowing that our faith does not rest upon human resources but in a God who raises the dead. We thank you in Jesus' name, Amen.

CHAPTER THIRTEEN

LAST WORDS
Acts 20:2-38

The good news about Jesus had changed the whole cultural pattern of the city of Ephesus and had destroyed the market for the silversmiths' souvenirs of the temple of Artemis. Luke picks up the account of Paul's ministry as he goes from Ephesus through Macedonia and into Greece:

> When he had gone through these parts and had given them much encouragement, he came to Greece. There he spent three months . . . (Acts 20:2, 3).

Paul moved through cities he had already visited, cities where he had founded churches—Philippi, Thessalonica, Berea—and he probably spoke to the believers in Athens. Finally he came to Corinth, where he stayed for the three months mentioned by Luke. It is amazing that Luke records so briefly a ministry which extended for a period of at least a year. Many incidents in the life of Paul which we would like to know about are simply not recorded. For example, he visited the region which today we call Albania and Yugoslavia. In those ancient times it was called Illyricum, and Paul refers to it briefly in the Book of Romans, but we know nothing of what happened there. One day it will be exciting to hear from his own lips about these forgotten parts of his ministry.

Traveling Seminary

He went into these areas, as we have said, in order to encourage the believers. Also, remember that Paul collected the contributions which the saints in these Gentile churches had made toward relief of the famished and poverty-stricken believers in Jerusalem. Several men were appointed by each church to travel with him and take these gifts to Jerusalem. Luke tells us who some of them were in the next section:

> There [in Corinth] he spent three months, and when a plot was made against him by the Jews as he was about to set sail for Syria, he determined to return through Macedonia. Sopater of Beroea, the son of Pyrrhus, accompanied him; and of the Thessalonians, Aristarchus and Secundus; and Gaius of Derbe, and Timothy; and the Asians, Tychicus and Trophimus. These went on and were waiting for us at Troas, but we sailed away from Philippi after the days of Unleavened Bread, and in five days we came to them at Troas, where we stayed for seven days (Acts 20:3-6).

Paul intended to sail directly from Corinth to Antioch and then on to Jerusalem, for he wanted to be there for the feast of the Passover. But he heard rumors of a plot against him, apparently involving the ship on which he was to sail. Very likely the Jews plotted that somewhere in the course of the voyage they would simply push him overboard and thus get rid of this man who, in their judgment, was very troublesome. But God was always alert to keep the apostle informed of these plots against him. So Paul changed his mind and went back through Macedonia, through Thessalonica and Philippi. There Luke joined them—notice the change from "them" to "us" in verse 5—and they sailed on together to Troas.

At Troas were waiting these young men whose names are mentioned, some of whom had once been slaves. The man whose name was Secundus, which means "the second," was obviously a slave. Slaves did not bother to name their children; they just numbered them—the first, the second, the third, and so on. It may be that "number three," Tertius, who wrote the Letter to the Romans as Paul's secretary, was this man's brother.

Paul insisted that these men go with him to Jerusalem in order to make sure that the funds were handled properly and that no one would misuse them in any way. But also, "coincidentally," these were sharp, alert young men, especially picked to travel with the apostle and to learn from him. So Paul had a traveling seminary and, as they went along by ship and by road, he taught these young men from the Scriptures.

Asleep in the Window

In the next paragraph we have an intimate glimpse of a wonderful event which occurred in Troas:

> On the first day of the week, when we were gathered together to break bread, Paul talked with them, intending to depart on the morrow; and he prolonged his speech until midnight. There were many lights in the upper chamber where we were gathered. And a

young man named Eutychus was sitting in the window. He sank into a deep sleep as Paul talked still
longer; and being overcome by sleep, he fell down
from the third story and was taken up dead. But Paul
went down and bent over him, and embracing him
said, "Do not be alarmed, for his life is in him" (Acts
20:7-10).

There are several very interesting aspects of this
story. This is the first mention we have of the worship of
the believers on the first day of the week. This early in
the Christian era they had shifted from Saturday for their
gathering, to Sunday, the first day of the week, the day of
our Lord's resurrection. They evidently had met here for
a communion service, and the apostle seized the occasion
to teach them from the Scriptures. He loved to teach the
Word because he knew it would deliver these people. He
had very little time to spend in Troas, but he did stay for
a week to teach them the delivering truth. In his last
evening there, before they gathered at the Lord's table,
he took time to teach them further from the Scriptures.
He went on at considerable length, prolonging his
speech until midnight.

This has always been an encouraging passage to any
pastor; even the Apostle Paul had people go to sleep on
him! Someone has said that the art of preaching is talking
in other people's sleep! At any rate, Eutychus fought a
losing battle against falling asleep. Luke, with his
physician's eye, is quick to make it as easy as possible on
him. He tells us that there were many lamps in the upper
chamber and each, of course, was burning up the oxygen.
So, with the loss of oxygen in the atmosphere and the late
hour and perhaps a long week's work behind him—as
well as Paul's long message—this young man was unable

to hold out. He was seated in the window and fell into a deep sleep—actually the Greek word is the one from which we derive "hypnosis"—and fell from the third floor.

Some people question whether he actually died. But the issue is settled by a physician's testimony. It is Luke who says that they took him up dead. So when Paul, going down and falling over him and embracing him, said, "Do not be alarmed, for his life is in him," he did not mean he was still alive. He meant that his life had *returned* to him. Thus he was really used of God in the great miracle of raising this young man from the dead.

Peter, of course, was involved in a similar miracle in the case of Dorcas, all the more remarkable because she had been dead for several hours by the time he prayed for her. The ministries of these mighty apostles of God were confirmed by unusual miracles, including this one of raising a young man from the dead.

We have another touching note at the close of the paragraph:

And when Paul had gone up and had broken bread and eaten, he conversed with them a long while, until daybreak, and so departed. And they took the lad away alive, and were not a little comforted (Acts 20:11, 12).

Evidently the communion service had been interrupted by this young man's "fall from grace," and when they had restored him they went back up and finished the Lord's supper. Then they enjoyed a wonderful time together in body life, conversing with one another, fellowshiping in the Lord, and sharing each others' experiences. So wonderful was this time that Paul could not tear himself away, even though he had a long walk ahead of him on the morrow. He stayed with them in fellowship all night, rejoicing at the restoring grace of God who had brought this young man back to life.

Now Luke continues the story:

But going ahead to the ship, we set sail for Assos, intending to take Paul aboard there; for so he had arranged, intending himself to go by land (Acts 20:13).

We are not told here why Paul chose this route. He sent them around a point that jutted into the sea, a voyage of about forty miles, while he cut across the neck of the peninsula, a hike of about twenty-five miles. He walked alone, very likely because he wanted to have time for meditation and prayer. He could walk and think and pray alone together with the Lord. This was also the habit of the Lord Jesus himself, who used to draw aside for times of meditation.

And when he met us at Assos, we took him on board and came to Mitylene. And sailing from there we came the following day opposite Chios; the next day we touched at Samos; and the day after that we came to Miletus. For Paul had decided to sail past Ephesus, so that he might not have to spend time in Asia; for he was hastening to be at Jerusalem, if possible, on the day of Pentecost. And from Miletus he sent to Ephesus and called to him the elders of the church (Acts 20:14-17).

It is evident that the apostle was trying to maintain a schedule. He had planned to be at Jerusalem for the Passover, but he had missed that, and so now he was trying to make it for the day of Pentecost, that day on which the Holy Spirit had first come to indwell the Christians many years before. He wanted to go there not only to be with the believers but to be with the Jews as well, to help them in their celebration of the feast day of Pentecost. He had never forgotten his Jewish ancestry and his love for the people of Israel, and he longed to reach them. And so, in order not to waste time, he sent to Ephesus and asked the elders to join him at the port city of Miletus, about fifteen miles from Ephesus. They came, and Paul met them with a great message about their ministry, which occupies the rest of this chapter.

Free to Make Plans

Some Christians are afraid to do any planning. They realize that God is in charge of their lives and they want to be available to do his will, so they often go to the extreme of never doing any planning at all. But notice here that the apostle does plan ahead, although he is ready for any change that God might make in his program. These early Christians understood that God left choices up to them. They were to think and dream, to plan and program, but, as James tells us, they were always to remember that God has the right to interrupt and to change those plans. This is where so many of us get frustrated. It is right to plan, but it is also right to always remember that God can change that plan, and that *his* plan is the important one. We are not to be frustrated or to feel that we are being imposed upon or mistreated because things do not go as we planned. The apostle never seemed to object when God changed the plan.

Now we come to Paul's great charge to the Ephesian

elders. In it the apostle is describing and defending his own ministry. It is a beautiful passage, from which we get perhaps the most intimate glimpse anywhere in the Scriptures of the heart of this great apostle, of the character of his labors, and of his concern for those with whom he ministers. We will examine it in sections, dividing it according to subject matter.

With Humility and Tears

The elders were what we would call the pastors of the churches there. In these ancient cities they did not meet together in church as we do on a Sunday morning. There was no room suitable for them to do so because there were probably thousands of Christians in Ephesus. They could not get together in one place, so they met in homes. In a letter to Corinth Paul speaks of the church in Ephesus which met at the house of Aquila and Priscilla, and there were many other house churches as well. The teachers of these various house-churches were the elders, those responsible for guiding and directing and teaching and feeding the flock. These are the men whom Paul has summoned to meet him at Miletus. He begins with a defense of his own ministry:

> And when they came to him, he said to them: "You yourselves know how I lived among you all the time from the first day that I set foot in Asia, serving the Lord with all humility and with tears and with trials which befell me through the plots of the Jews . . ." (Acts 20:18, 19).

Some people read Paul's message and feel that he is

being very conceited about his own ministry, that he is speaking at length of how he suffered but was faithful, and of how he preached the Word with power. They say he is very much aware of his own success. But if you understand that by this time the apostle is under attack and that his ministry is being threatened, you will know why he addresses a defense of his ministry to these people.

In what way is he being attacked? He says that he preached with humility and with tears and went through trials which befell him through the plots of the Jews. This implies that his enemies were suggesting that he was proud, the opposite of humble, and that he was insincere, superficial, and a troublemaker, stirring up dissension everywhere he went. But Paul says, "No, I served the Lord with humility and with tears. This ministry meant everything to me. I wasn't insincere. And the trouble was caused by the Jews, not by me."

In the next section we have the manner of his ministry—a wonderful glimpse of how he worked:

". . . how I did not shrink from declaring to you anything that was profitable, and teaching you in public and from house to house, testifying both to Jews and to Greeks of repentance to God and of faith in our Lord Jesus Christ" (Acts 20:20, 21).

Whenever Paul came into these cities, he always sought first to set forth the whole counsel of God. He tried to teach the people the whole truth; he didn't want them to be shortchanged in any way. Sometimes Paul stayed up long hours in order to cover all that God has said to man, because he knew and understood that it is the knowledge of the Word that sets people free.

I wish I could make this clear to people who are struggling with problems and internal tensions and pressures, and with boredom, frustration, and a sense of restlessness—all the negative qualities of life. God has never intended for you to live like that. That is why he has given you the Word. It is the Word of truth that sets you free. When you learn it and understand it and operate on it, it will always set you free.

Walk and Words

This is why Paul emphasized this ministry so strongly. He was faithful in its delivery not only in public but also from house to house, testifying of it everywhere. Also, see how practical it was. It could always be reduced to two concepts: repentance toward God and faith toward our Lord Jesus Christ. There is the Christian message, summarized for us very neatly in two words: repent and believe. These two basic steps relate not only to the beginning of the Christian life but also to our walk throughout the Christian life. A walk is more than a single step. When faced with a situation, you should take the first step and repent, think through the old way of life and say to yourself, "I've been going at this the wrong way." But that is not yet a walk. You must take the next step and believe, have faith, trust in the work of God in you. Then, on the next occasion that comes, you go through the same procedure over again—you repent, and then believe—repent and believe—repent and believe—and you are walking! That is what the Christian life is all about. In every circumstance, every situation, this is the twofold way by which the Christian lives in the power of a living God: repent and believe.

Now the apostle goes on to give another characteristic of his ministry among them:

And now, behold, I am going to Jerusalem, bound in the Spirit, not knowing what shall befall me there, except that the Holy Spirit testifies to me in every city that imprisonment and afflictions await me. But I do not account my life of any value nor as precious to myself, if only I may accomplish my course and the ministry which I received from the Lord Jesus, to testify to the gospel of the grace of God. And now, behold, I know that all you among whom I have gone about preaching the kingdom will see my face no more. Therefore I testify to you this day that I am innocent of the blood of all of you, for I did not shrink from declaring to you the whole counsel of God (Acts 20:22-27).

What a magnificent statement! Note how costly Paul's ministry is. He knows that he is facing danger, trial, hardship, affliction. Everywhere he had gone, the Holy Spirit had witnessed to him through circumstances and through other Christians that he was heading for trouble, and he knew it. But note also the commitment of his heart. He says that it does not matter. Karl Marx wrote that Communists are dead men on furlough, i.e., they treat themselves as though they are as good as dead. They have nothing to lose, so they are ready for anything. That characterizes even better what a Christian is. He is *really* a dead man on furlough. He wants nothing for himself, but wants only to have God exalted, Christ manifested. Paul says, "I do not count my life of any value nor as precious to myself—I am not my own, but I am bought with a price. And that purchase means that I am available to Another to work through me. My aim, my goal, my joy, my desire in life is not that I should have anything for myself, but for my Lord." What a wonderful statement of how available he was as an instrument of God's working!

Then Paul makes very clear that he is aware that he has completed his ministry among them: "I testify to you that I am innocent of the blood of all of you, for I have declared to you the whole counsel of God. I have not kept anything back. I have given you the truth. You have listened to it, you have heard it, you know what God has to say. You know the provision for his working, you know the power available to you, you know how to live in a way that will please God and will fulfill your humanity. Now it is up to you; the decision is yours. Now move out upon the truth you know, because there is nothing further that I can do."

The Authority of Obedience

In the final section Paul goes briefly into the responsibilities of these elders to the flock at Ephesus. There are three considerations which the apostle wants to lay before them to govern them in their ministry, and the first is to feed the flock:

> **Take heed to yourselves and to all the flock, in which the Holy Spirit has made you guardians [or overseers, pastors], to feed the church of the Lord which he obtained with his own blood (Acts 20:28).**

The primary responsibility of a pastor is to teach the Scriptures, to feed the flock. If he is not doing that, he is miserably failing in his job. If the Word, the Scripture, is not being taught, then people are not being changed. They are struggling on in their own futile ways and nothing is being accomplished. So the primary job of pastors is to set the whole counsel of God before the people.

They are to begin with themselves, however; that is, they are to obey the truth which they teach. This is where their authority comes from; it is only as they are obedient to the truth which they teach that they have any right to say anything to anyone else. Even the Lord Jesus operated on that basis. He said to his disciples on one occasion, "If I do not the works of my father, then don't believe me." That is, if what I am doing is not in exact accord with what I am saying, then don't believe me!" Would you dare say that to your children? Or to your Sunday school class? Or to others who observe you as a Christian? "If what I am doing is not in line with what I teach, then don't believe me. I have no authority over you; I have no power over you." But if your actions are in accord with your teaching then power is inherent in that obedience.

So these elders are to begin with themselves, and to teach the Word. Their responsibility is to the Holy Spirit, not to the denomination or to the congregation. It is the Spirit who has set them in that office and has equipped them with gifts. He who reads the heart is judging their lives, so it doesn't make any difference what anybody else thinks. They are responsible to follow the Holy Spirit in what he has given them to do.

Notice how Paul underscores the fact that theirs is a very precious ministry. It is to feed the church of the Lord. Nothing is more precious to God in all the world than the people of Christ, the body of Christ. The most valuable thing on earth, in God's sight, is his church. He gave himself for it, he loves it earnestly, "he obtained it with his own blood." Therefore it has highest priority in his schedule and emphasis. What concerns the church is the most important thing in the world today. I wish we could catch that picture as the apostle understood it.

The second thing Paul exhorts them to do is to watch for perils:

I know that after my departure fierce wolves will come in among you, not sparing the flock; and from among your own selves will arise men speaking perverse things, to draw away the disciples after them (Acts 20:29, 30).

There will be two sources of danger, Paul says. The first is that impostors like wolves will come in among the believers. Jesus said that too. Wolves in sheep's clothing, unregenerate men and women who talk and act like Christians and perhaps even think they are Christians, but who are not born again, will come into the church. They will be religious but will deny the power of true faith, and they will disturb and divide and ruin the church of God. These words have been fulfilled throughout the centuries, many times over.

But also from within themselves, from among the elders, the leaders, will arise men who will teach distorted doctrines. The danger, again, will be that they will divide people, separate them, form little cliques which gather around particular leaders. Instead of uniting people in the fellowship of the body they will separate them out into special little groups which follow one man's view and turn away from others. Through the centuries these are the things which have disturbed the church of God.

Fire and Brimstone with Love

The third consideration which Paul lays before the Ephesian elders is to do all this in the spirit which he himself has exemplified:

> Therefore be alert, remembering that for three years I did not cease night or day to admonish everyone with tears. And now I commend you to God and to the word of his grace, which is able to build you up and to give you the inheritance among all those who are sanctified. I coveted no one's silver or gold or apparel. You yourselves know that these hands ministered to my necessities, and to those who were with me. In all things I have shown you that by so toiling one must help the weak, remembering the words of the Lord Jesus, how he said, "It is more blessed to give than to receive (Acts 20:31-35).

The apostle himself has been their example. They are to perform this ministry in four ways. The first is by admonishing with tears, or, as Paul writes later to the Ephesians, by speaking the truth in love. I heard the other day of a certain church which had dismissed its pastor and gotten a new one. Someone asked why they had gotten rid of the old one. A spokesman said, "Because he kept telling the people they were going to hell." The questioner asked, "What does the new man say?" "Oh, he keeps telling them they're going to hell, too." "Well, what is the difference?" he was asked. He replied, "The difference is that when the first one said it, he sounded as if he were glad of it. But when the second one says it, he lets you know it is breaking his heart." That is the difference the apostle is talking about— admonishing with tears, not with harshness, not with judgment, but with concern and care and love, speaking the truth in love.

The second way is to use the Word. "I commend you to the Word," he said. "You have all you need in that. It is able to do what it was sent to do. It is able to build you up and give you the inheritance provided for you, the inheritance of the saints in Jesus Christ—all that Christ is, made available to you."

And thirdly, Paul says, "Be selfless in your ministry. Do not be looking for something for yourself, do not be seeking glory for yourself, or favor, or position, or eminence, or prominence, or material reward. Look at me," he says. "I have labored among you and these hands have made tents to pay for my basic needs." Finally, "Remember that the Lord Jesus has said, 'It is better to give than to receive.' So labor hard in order that you may be able to give and thus to receive the better reward."

The last paragraph hardly needs comment. It describes the beautiful farewell service of parting:

And when he had spoken thus, he knelt down and prayed with them all. And they all wept and embraced Paul and kissed him, sorrowing most of all because of the word he had spoken, that they should see his face no more. And they brought him to the ship (Acts 20:36-38).

I'm glad that Paul was wrong about this. They *did* see his face again. In First Timothy we learn that he paid another visit to Ephesus after this one. But he didn't know this at the time, so they all thought this was their last glimpse of their beloved leader. What a touching scene this was as they fellowshiped together, facing the dangers that lay ahead but strengthening one another in the Lord—undergirding, supporting, praying for one another, feeling the heartache of the occasion and yet the joy of sharing together in the life of Jesus Christ.

Our heavenly Father, how grateful we are for your Word. How much it speaks to our hearts! How powerful is its ministry to us! And, in the hands of the Spirit, how graciously it teaches us, especially through the other members of the body. Unite us together, Lord, in love for one another. As we face the uncertainties, dangers, afflictions, hardships, and possibilities of our lives, we pray, Lord, that we may do so with a sense of our need for each other, and of our need for you above all else. We pray that you will sustain us and strengthen us and, as is your wont, that you will surprise us with such moments of joy which it is your delight to give to us. We thank you in Jesus' name, Amen.

Christian Marriage

by Dr. Howard Hendricks

As most couples soon discover, marriage is only as durable as its foundation, and as flexible as its participants. In this fascinating guide to the Christian perspective of marriage, Dr. Hendricks demonstrates the clear relationship between faith in God and marital depth and harmony.

Tape Titles:
What is Love? · Foundations of a Christian Marriage · Communication or Chaos · Purpose of Sex in Marriage · The Role and Responsibility of the Husband · The Role and Responsibility of the Wife

6 tapes available separately $34.98

Preparing for Adolescence Growthguide
A delightfully illustrated workbook of discussion-provoking ideas, plus self-tests and projects designed to encourage the teenager to think through important issues about himself and his beliefs.
Paper $4.95

Preparing for Adolescence cassettes
In the following six cassettes, he speaks directly to the pre-teenager in a friendly, casual manner. This portion of the series is available separately —already a best-selling album for individual use with pre-teens... in group discussions... in pastoral counseling.
Tape titles: "I Wish I Were Somebody Else" Self Esteem and How to Keep It · "I Think I've Fallen in Love" Understanding the Real Meaning of Love · "But Everybody's Doing It" Group Pressure and How to Handle It · "What Else Should I Know?" Introducing You to Yourself · "Something Crazy Is Happening to My Body" Understanding Physical and Sexual Development · "This Is How It Was with Me" Rap Session with Four Teenagers.
6 Tapes $34.98

Preparing for Adolescence Pak

Includes...
■ **Eight cassettes** In addition to the six tapes described above, Dr. Dobson has included two cassettes for parents and leaders. Pertinent guidelines to encourage adolescents through a meaningful program.

■ **Book**
■ **Growthguide** (See above)
Only $59.95

From the Heart of Joyce Landorf

Joyce presents sparkling highlights from her best-selling books. The following four cassettes are also available as singles, for $5.98 each.
4 Tapes $24.98

The Fragrance of Beauty ▪ Skillfully shows how to achieve an inner beauty that outglows all others.

His Stubborn Love ▪ Joyce shares the reality of a marriage on the rocks as well as the answers she and her husband found with God's help. These same answers may well improve your marriage.

Mourning Song ▪ With great sensitivity, Joyce talks about the tremendous trial of accepting one's own approaching death or that of a close family member. A truly inspirational and strengthening message.

The Richest Lady in Town ▪ Most women are passing up the wealth available through Christ as they seek artificial solutions to problems of personal fulfillment.

CASSETTES

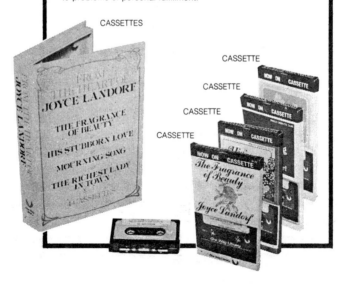

For These Fragile Times ■ At a time when human relationships are so easily shattered comes this cheerful message. Let Joyce tell you how life with those around you can become exciting and new! A refreshing breakthrough for developing lasting relationships. *Single Cassette $5.98*

Dinner Hour: Disaster or Delight ■ Don't let family feuds spoil another carefully planned and lovingly prepared dinner! Joyce offers hints for making mealtimes pleasant, sharing experiences for all family members. Bring your family together at the table tonight! *Single Cassette $5.98*

Tough and Tender ■ Joyce directs this message to men—as only a very sensitive and sensible wife and mother can. She's down to earth about the responsibilities of spiritual leadership in the home, and about "tuning in" to the daily considerations that can strengthen every marriage relationship. Every woman wants and can have a man that's tough and tender. *Single Cassette $5.98*

CASSETTE

CASSETTE

CASSETTE